# What is Existentialism?

# What is Existentialism?

*by William Barrett*

GROVE PRESS, INC.     NEW YORK

# Contents

# Foreword

THE QUESTION What is Existentialism? hardly raises the same journalistic titter of excitement that it once did. Curiosity on the subject has not ceased; on the whole, I would say that it has become more widespread and steadier—and, I believe, much more serious. When people ask the question now, they no longer want tidbits of gossip about a literary school in Paris in the late 1940's. For good or ill, existentialism has taken an acknowledged place among the more significant modes of thought within the modern world.

The two parts of this book are separated by more than a dozen years, yet they revolve around the same themes and are troubled by the same problems. The differences between them the reader will easily perceive for himself. I myself, in re-reading them, am more surprised by their continuity than by their divergences. Neither tries to give any neat encapsulated definition of existentialism. The aim rather is to tell something about this philosophy by plunging the reader into some of the problems that the existentialists have dealt with.

The first part originated at the time when the French

7

existentialists were just becoming known here. Camus's *The Stranger* had just been translated, and two of Sartre's plays —*No Exit* and *The Flies*—had been produced in New York. At the time I was on the staff of *Partisan Review* and very much immersed in the French writers; my fellow editors suggested that since there was a public need to know what existentialism was, I should be the one to attempt the explanation. The result is the first part of this book, which, born under the particular pressures of that moment, reflects the intellectual mood of its period.

Perhaps the classic expression of that mood is still Meursault, the hero of *The Stranger*. Though this novel was a very personal expression for Camus himself, its hero is none the less a literary archetype of the alienated man, at once the filial descendant of the outcasts of Dostoevsky and Kafka, and a prophet of the leather-jacketed Beats who were not to appear for another decade. Though Meursault begins as a little man of no importance, a clerk caught in the absurd lockstep of society, he nevertheless achieves a certain grandeur and heroism toward the end, when in the courageous confrontation of his death he becomes authentically human. This novel is hardly the greatest treatment of alienation in Western literatures, yet Camus did add something of great significance to the Russians and Kafka: a French lucidity and logic that expresses its material with thematic clarity. These themes—the incurable isolation of the individual, the absurd mechanisms of society that destroy him, and the courage to face death while affirming life—have been persistent ones in existentialism, or at least *one* side of existentialism.

The other side of existentialism is not a question of literary sensibility at all but of philosophy itself. The matters that concern the existentialists concern all men, and therefore the professional philosopher too. But the latter, in turn, has the right of the specialist to ask whether this philosophy does add some significantly new perspective to Western thought. If a philosophy has something new to say, then the whole history of philosophy becomes altered. From the beginning, then, I was not so much interested in reporting a current postwar mood in France, but in placing existentialist thought within the stream of history—in relation, first, to other contemporary philosophizing, and, then, more broadly within Western culture since the movement of romanticism. In those early days, too, I was convinced that Heidegger was, philosophically speaking, the key to this movement. If his thinking does come to anything, then it *may* mark (one has to insist on the uncertain and problematical "may") a change in philosophy comparable in its decisiveness to that given by Hegel.

Hegel, indeed, is the perplexing figure for the history of existentialism; and if I were to change in any significant way my earlier essay, it would be in enlarging his philosophical role in this movement. To be sure, the stock Hegel is real enough in his own writings and in the image projected by some of his followers. This is the arch rationalist who believed that the real is rational and the rational alone is fully real, and who sought to enclose all of human existence in his system. And, of course, it is against this Hegel that Kierkegaard revolted in the name of our poor, tattered, finite, fragmentary, and quite unsystematic human exist-

ence. And so, it is said, existentialism began. True enough;
but there is another side to Hegel, which nowadays absorbs
my attention more than it once did.

The fact is that Hegel is a philosopher very much divided
against himself. He is at once the last and the first—the last
audacious representative of classical rationalism, and the first
pioneer of a new historical mode of thought. In a good deal
of Hegel, Reason itself plays second fiddle to Spirit (*Geist*);
and Spirit, he insists, must be understood concretely and historically. He wrote many intoxicated and mystifying words
about Spirit, but the main outline of what he wanted to say
seems to me tolerably clear. To begin with, Spirit is what
distinguishes man from the animal, and so represents the full
content of our humanity. But it can only be understood
concretely as it objectifies itself in human institutions, laws,
customs, art and poetry—as well as in the sciences and philosophy. Hegel here immerses man within history with a
completeness beyond any previous thinker. Even today, for
example, it is not usually perceived that his *Philosophy of
Art* really rejects aesthetics as a discipline supposed to reveal
the eternal truths about art, and substitutes for it the philosophical history of art. That is to say, the comprehension of
any human product requires that we grasp it within the unfolding pattern of history.

It is but one step, and not a long one at that, from this
Hegelian insistence on the essentially historical character of
the human spirit to the existentialist slogan: "Man has no
nature, but only a history." For if the human spirit exists
only in so far as it externalizes itself in the social forms of
art, law, and customs, then the very content of our humanity lies in the accumulated and evolving fabrications of

history itself. Man is what he is through a history that he himself makes. A human nature, outside of history, selfsame and eternal, is an idea empty of content. Such are the sweeping and drastic conclusions from Hegel's doctrine of Spirit. And in this respect he might be said to have originated existentialism. His rebellious sons—Marx, Kierkegaard, and Nietzsche—could not have accomplished what they did without the father whom they professed to be turning on his head.

Hegel himself did not see that this radically historical point of view introduced an unresolvable discord into the system because he was still sustained by a brave faith in the ultimate harmony of things. Though he was indefatigable in searching out all the tragedies, conflicts, and discords of history, he seemed always to hear the resolving chords in the background. A comparison here with Beethoven is not at all farfetched; and perhaps Hegel himself, who believed in the power of the *Zeitgeist*, could he look back now, would welcome the parallel. Both men were born in the same year (1770), and their lives spanned almost the same years (Beethoven died in 1827, Hegel in 1831). Beethoven, as compared with his musical predecessors, contrived unusual dissonances, unexpected modulations and progressions. Some musicians even profess to see in his last works the beginning of atonal music. But however imperious the conflict raging within any of his symphonies, in the end the resolving harmony always sounds. So too with the symphony of history that Hegel created. The Spirit can always return to its home in the tonic. But where such a richness of discord exists, one has only to take the next step and the safe harbor of tonality vanishes; and with this, the predictable chords that will resolve everything. This is what happened in music. And something very like it began to happen in philosophy after Hegel.

Since Hegel, our philosophers have been thinking, so to speak, atonally. When the grand harmonies are gone, many people will recoil from a world that strikes them as one of mere shards and fragments. Many of the popular complaints against existentialism, when it first became known in this country, were provoked by the unpleasant and discordant realities it talked about that people would prefer to forget. Such complaints seem to me to have as much justice as the criticisms of composers simply for writing atonal music at all. If we live in an atonal world, we have to learn to make our music atonally. And we have to learn to think in accordance with that world too.

WILLIAM BARRETT

New York
1963

# Part 1

# WHAT IS EXISTENTIALISM?

*We have ambiguous relations to the nineteenth century. For at least two decades, maybe more, we have felt ourselves from time to time, and more or less consciously, in revolt against it. But the revolt is a little like that of a rebellious son against his father: the more concentrated and sharp his opposition the more he begins to discover in himself possible resemblances to the parent—his voice, his gestures, features that stare back at him from the mirror—all of which makes him more deeply uneasy, and only serves to sharpen the fury of his rebellion. For, after all, what is his revolt for except to be himself, to have a mind of his own?*

*Indeed, that century has so many aspects that all we are, and have, seems to be found there—at least in germ. It contains positivism; but shortly before he publishes his* Course in Positive Philosophy, *August Comte spends a year in an insane asylum. Curious contrast of light and shadow! The century contains Macaulay, very much at ease in Sion, prophet of liberal enlightenment and progress; and in 1851 London exults in what seems almost the architectural embodiment of his voice: the Crystal Palace of the International Exposition. But far away in Russia this Crystal Palace evokes a strange comment, and a stranger commentator: Dostoevsky's Underground Man.*

*He seems to haunt that century. He is the bad breath that*

*one sniffs behind the smile and clear even teeth—a little like
that odor of death that Céline (our twentieth-century incarnation of the Underground Man) smelled from the
mouths of the poor. But perhaps the Underground Man has
as much to teach us as the Crystal Palace. A wise French
critic (who is not an existentialist, beyond being a disciple
of Montaigne) has said:* "Man has that in him which sometimes rejects the sun or his neighbors, and vomits out the
State, nature, all logic and common sense." *The Underground Man does not miss any of these rejections. He
vomits up the State:*

New economic relations will be established, worked out with
mathematical exactitude, so that every possible question will
vanish. Then the "Palace of Crystal" will be built. Of course
there is no guaranteeing that it will not be frightfully dull then,
but on the other hand everything will be frightfully rational.
Of course boredom may lead you to anything. It is boredom
sets one to sticking pins into people.

*He vomits up nature and reason:*

But what do I care for the laws of nature and arithmetic, when,
for some reason, I dislike those laws and the fact that twice two
makes four?

*Indeed, he is capable of vomiting up everything the nine-
teenth century was able, for a while, to believe in.*

*Here a scandal has broken out, we can no longer hide it,
there are outcries and a great clatter in the market place.
When we look back on it now, the whole century was
struggling to exorcise this unpleasant shade.* "I can enclose
him in the System," *says Hegel.* "Let him make the religious
leap with me and he will be saved" *(Kierkegaard). Or:*

*"We must overcome and subdue this Nihilist, but we have first to live through his experience to the end"* (Nietzsche). *Or a clipped and cooler English voice: "He is no gentleman"* (Macaulay). *And so on and so forth.*

*Now I have no new proposal as to what is to be done with this Underground Man. Perhaps he is not demanding a new truth at all, but only that truth should take some notice of his own concrete existence, with its aching liver, its humiliations and resentments. I only wish to plant him here because he sets a tone, because it is convenient to have him here for later reference—as one might post an unpleasant beggar, a poor relation of the family, at the doorway, ready to be called in when one has to make a point very emphatically to the family inside.*

# I

## Who is "Existential"?

A FEW YEARS AGO, after the liberating armies swept into Paris and the veil separating France from us was lifted, so that we could find out at last what the French had been doing culturally during the dark years of the war, a curious phenomenon took place in New York—so closely bound together is the modern world. People began speaking of philosophical matters in the most unexpected places. One might almost have believed—for a moment—that in America people think. It was a triumph for French culture to make the art world of Fifty-seventh Street, as well as the fashion world of *Vogue* magazine, talk philosophy. Existential philosophy had acquired the voice of French eloquence, and it was something to be assimilated along with French painting, millinery, and literature, endowed with the charms of Gallic taste and *finesse*.

We have no objection at all to the fact that Fifty-seventh Street (or any other street, for that matter) should begin to talk philosophy. Indeed, one of the signs of the decay of modern academic philosophy has been its inability to create more than a whisper outside its own classrooms, much less go out into the streets. Nevertheless the present vogue of French existentialism does create a certain embarrassment in some of us, for like all fashions this too often seeks the adventitious, the easy and sensational, obscuring the long and serious past required to produce these words that are now thrown around like slogans. We become a little embarrassed at the word "existential" altogether—though it had known a very common and widespread use in modern philosophy before the works of Sartre become fashionable property. Not to mention the fact that there are a good many people who naturally suspect a philosophy that is able to make the pages of the women's fashion magazines.

But despite some accompanying aberrations, the present French movement is serious, it is genuinely at work on a subject matter, and it seeks to discover and assimilate something of its tradition. The immediate line of descent of this tradition may be traced quite simply. Existentialism, more or less in its present form, was produced in Germany after the first World War by two professors of philosophy, Karl Jaspers and Martin Heidegger. Their direct spiritual ancestor was a strange, captivating, and quite unclassifiable Dane, Sören Kierkegaard (1813–1855), most of whose important writings appeared in the 1840's. Kierkegaard himself has left us a charming account of the incident that launched him on his philosophical career, and for our present historical sketch it will do as a point of beginning. While he sat at the café in the Frederiksberg Garden in Copenhagen one afternoon, smoking a cigar, as was his habit, and turning over a great many things in his mind, Kierkegaard reflected that he had not really begun any career for himself, while a good many of his friends were already making names for themselves, getting set up in business or getting published, explaining everything in the philosophic mode of Hegel, which was then the reigning fashion. The cigar burned down, he lit another, the train of reflection held him. It occurred to him then that since everyone was engaged everywhere in making things easy, perhaps someone was needed to make things hard again, and that this too might be a career and a destiny—to go in search of difficulties, like a new Socrates. As for these difficulties, he did not have to go very far to find them: there was, for example, his own concrete existence, with all its passion and anxieties, its painful choices, which involved always a pathos of renunciation of which the Hegelian philosophy seemed to take no account. So Kierkegaard was launched upon his career, and the rest of his life was consumed in the continuous deed of existential thinking. Eventually, his writings were translated into German around the turn of the century, but they did not find their really fertile soil until the period following 1918, when they were taken up systematically by Jaspers and Heidegger. In France, the impact of Kierkegaard was not experienced until the thirties. About that time Heidegger too was translated into French and met a favorable reception from the young intellectuals nauseated by French bourgeois civilization on the eve of Munich. But it required another postwar climate—World War II, this time—for existentialism to take on the dimensions almost of a popular movement, whose high priest became the energetic Jean-Paul Sartre.

We travel a long road from Frederiksberg Garden, Copenhagen, to Fifty-seventh Street, New York. Strange things can happen when one lights a cigar.

Unfortunately for any such simple outline, history is never a matter of such direct filiations. We hardly trace a branch by following the single outline itself without reference to the trunk from which it springs and the other branches that bend it with them as they struggle together toward the same sunlight. Every idea comes into being at its own particular time, with all the pressures of this time upon it, and the less superficial it is the deeper its correspondences with the other ideas germinating in the same period. So we look beyond the many schools to the single tendency that unites them like so many isolated points on a curve; the tendency breaks down into issues, and these issues return us always to men, bound together in a particular historical epoch, facing the same world with the urgency of the same problems. Existentialism could be examined as just another philosophic school, one among many; but its full significance is disclosed only when we see it as a particular offshoot of a much broader and more complex existential tendency within modern philosophy as a whole.

It requires only a rapid glance over the philosophy of the last hundred years to discover in its development a remarkable enlargement of content, a progressive orientation toward the immediate and qualitative, the existent and factual —"concreteness and adequacy," to use Whitehead's pregnant words. The mention of Whitehead places us immediately within a circle of different names and influences. William James with his radical pluralism at the turn of the century, Bergson with his intuition, Whitehead with his doctrine of feeling—all bear witness to the same general direction. James, in turn, brings to mind John Dewey, and we recall that Dewey stood in the philosophic pillory for some of his earlier pragmatic writings while charges of "anti-rationalist" were hurled at him. Dewey had insisted on an existential context of thought, and some philosophers had cried out, scandalized, as if a finger had been pointed at their nakedness. Nietzsche had already pointed a more shocking and scandalizing finger at this philosophic nakedness. (And he had only the dream, the daring guess, of psychoanalysis, where we have now the rudiments of a science, so that we may be tempted shortly to a more systematic rudeness than his.) Thus, letting our circle widen, we pass from name to name, where the possibility of direct influence, as a simple linear filiation, is no longer in question.

The deeper historical reality here is not a mere matter of philosophic schools, or isolated figures extracting explicit nuggets of "influence" from one another, but the fact that the whole Western mind is bending before a new climate of opinion; as the biologist portrays a whole species, scattered in space and without contact, moving along the same paths of adaptation before a new geological upheaval. We could multiply correlations in this direction, but perhaps none lends more striking confirmation to our historical grouping than the comparison of Dewey with Wilhelm Dilthey*:

---

* Wilhelm Dilthey (1833–1911) taught at the universities of Basel, Kiel, Breslau, but his final, and most influential, post as teacher was at Berlin during the last years of his life. His fame was confined more or less to a small inner circle during his life. Ortega y Gasset recounts that when he was a student of philosophy in Germany in 1906 he had not yet heard the name of Dilthey, who was then in fact still teaching at Berlin. Yet Dilthey's stature has grown slowly and steadily since his

following an altogether different voyage of discovery, Dilthey came into sight of the same new-found land—the great
intuition that human thinking, philosophy included, arises

---

death, and some translations of his writings are beginning to appear in
English.

Dilthey began his philosophic career as an idealist, intending to
write a critique of historical knowledge that would do for this field
what Kant had accomplished in relation to the physical sciences.
Gradually, he was drawn into minute and detailed historical studies,
in which he became more and more impressed with the correlations
between the various expressions of culture—the art, religion, and
philosophical world-views—within a given period. The great synoptic
work toward which he aspired never got written. Yet from his tentative and groping explorations of history a great new insight was in-
sinuated, if never explicitly expressed in philosophic terms: namely,
of man as a creature time-bound in his historical situation, which im-
parts its stamp to every one of his cultural expressions. Dilthey is thus
a link between Hegel and Heidegger. On the one hand, he produced a
documentation to confirm Hegel's view of the Time-spirit (*Zeitgeist*)
as the conditioning factor in human history; on the other hand, he prepared the way for Heidegger's descriptions of man as the creature perpetually bound within his own finite historical horizons.

Yet Heidegger has had some harsh words for Dilthey. From Heidegger's point of view, the presuppositions of Dilthey's thinking have
remained entirely too subjectivistic. In *Being and Time* (1927) he
clothes his reservations on Dilthey's thinking with politeness. But elsewhere he has expressed himself more strongly. He has said that it is
something of a scandal that Hermann Diels's *Fragments of the Pre-
Socratics*, the text which provides us with our chief knowledge of the
early Greek thinkers, should be dedicated to Wilhelm Dilthey. A
scandal? Well, from Heidegger's point of view, certainly a curious
irony. Dilthey's personality was permeated by an excessively subjective and excessively cultured humanism; the thought of the early
Greeks was entirely foreign to such things. Yet there is another irony
to this dedication on which Heidegger might have pondered: Dilthey
had been such a stimulus to historical studies that the great scholar,
Diels, could think of no more worthy a name to whom to dedicate
his great work. In this case both Diels and Heidegger are right: in our
time it may require the most cultivated and over-refined to point the
way toward the primal sources of Being, which is what the early
Greek thinkers are.

within the context of a definite cultural existence, which at once sets philosophy its problems and defines its ultimate horizons. What had seemed a single branch has already broken out into a cluster, and we have now to thread our way through this greater density in search of the line of development in relation to which each of these philosophic shoots has its own grade of relevance.

The past is never given as finished and fixed, we are remaking it at every moment, and nowhere more than in that peculiarly fluent and plastic subject matter: the history of ideas. The order we impose upon the history of thought is modified by the entrance of new elements within that order. The names of Kierkegaard, Heidegger, and Jaspers are just beginning to be known in America. Once we admit these figures within our perspective on modern thought, this perspective itself becomes altered, and we see other issues at work below the surface of that past whose main lines had been taken as fixed and given. When William James objected to Hegel's universe on the ground that it reminded him of a seaside boarding house—a world without privacy, in which he felt faintly suffocated—he was making the kind of personal and passionate argument that we find everywhere in the pages of Kierkegaard. Only the convinced Hegelian might object that this is a personal remark and not a philosophic argument at all. James's point may be that there is no very great difference after all—that there can be no real separation between himself as man and himself as thinker, so that he could not, as philosopher, accept any elaborate view of the universe which he could not live with as a concrete existent being. Having read Kierkegaard, we can now see more clearly what was at issue in James's rejection of idealism. What James had seen with his psychologist's eye, delicately attentive to the variety and flux of experience, Kierkegaard had carried further toward explicitness as a philosophic principle. Where do we find this principle?

Walking around our subject for the moment, taking its measure from the outside like the invader surveying the city into which he would penetrate, we may begin from what is an external, but not therefore superficial, aspect: the language and style of this philosophy. Certainly, there is something historically remarkable in the way this philosophy is being written. Kierkegaard and Nietzsche, both literary geniuses, adopt the decision to communicate their thought indirectly, by fragments and aphorisms, and in both the philosophic expression hovers always on the edge of lyricism. Literary eloquence is never completely absent from the pages of James or Bergson, and often moves into the high gear of rhapsody. Whitehead fabricates a tremendous and orotund rhetoric, which is necessary more for expressive than analytic purposes. Heidegger develops a language of Gothic heaviness, lumbering under its weight of jargon and coinage, but in his use of it he often attains an extraordinary degree of expressiveness. Even Dewey, who would seem to be without literary pretensions altogether, nevertheless produces, in a book like *Experience and Nature*, a curious linguistic phenomenon: a language amorphous, halting, groping—as if he were trying to convince us of pragmatism by presenting us his thought in the very process of its making. When we come to the present existentialist school in France, we find the frontiers between philosophy and literature at the point of disappearing altogether: the nature of human existence would seem to be such that it compels philosophers to write novels, plays, and literary criticism.

One might at first be suspicious, and even not pass beyond the suspicion, that we have here only a fundamental confusion of genres. But the miscegenation of literary genres in the past has often brought forth a really new kind of expression and even new kinds of consciousness; and philosophy itself has performed many of its historical services, whether or not the eventual specialization of the human mind will dispense with these, as a rather uncertain hybrid of poetry and science. At some levels of experience the distinction between the expressive and analytic uses of language may break down or become unusable. We do not know, but in any case some modern philosophers have become so possessed by the vision of the existent in its concreteness and immediacy, that this has got into their language, which struggles to *present* the reality that they seek to understand. This quality of language immediately marks off this tendency from another that is equally characteristic of modern philosophy. What is now called analytic philosophy has proceeded in the opposite direction, toward greater abstractness, a purification and precision of language, formalism, symbolic language. The result is that philosophers in one group have largely ceased to understand those in the other. Philosophy seems well on its way toward the schizophrenic split that, in other forms and on other levels, has become the common experience of our culture. The dangers of this split, which are grave for both sides, we need not go into here; we point to it only in order to demarcate the broader existential tendency against the contrasting background of another large-scale modern movement. And we have only to turn our attention to the language in which the philosopher of the eighteenth century expressed himself to see how the style and expression of these moderns also defines them against the background of the past. When a literary note creeps into a philosopher like Kant, it is only by way of an occasional and extraneous flourish or metaphor, by which, paying his respects to the eighteenth-century humanities, he punctuates the straightforward bald presentation of his argument.

All this adds up to the fact that we may now isolate a single tendency of philosophy during the last hundred years and place it against the background of the whole of Western philosophy, taken as a unit, from Descartes to Kant. The first, the immediately obvious characteristic of this tendency, is that through it philosophy has experienced an extraordinary widening and enrichment of data. From Descartes to Kant, man was taken fundamentally as a perceiving-thinking animal, a mechanical body plus a conscious soul. This was the traditional inheritance from the Greeks, who had defined man as essentially the rational animal, but a tradition now running thin, having lost all its original overtones from Greek religion, poetry, and society. Other regions of man's being fall within the experience of the Christian religion, but in this period philosophy separates itself from positive religion. In the seventeenth century this rational soul falls within the framework of a universe whose basic features are expressed by the physical notions of Newton. The fundamental key to the human situation becomes the relation of the rational soul to this inertly material universe: man becomes the epistemological animal. But bit by bit the developments of history complicate this simple picture: new sources of information, new regions of experience and feeling, enrich and complicate the philosopher's view of the human situation. Reason itself can no longer be looked upon as the simple faculty of a soul or mind; viewed concretely, it shows itself as a complicated structure evolved by culture and history, as, in the sphere of morals, the complexity of the superego takes the place of the older simple "moral sense." Now, up to a certain point the enrichment of data takes place within the old framework, each detail filling in an empty space on a canvas that is completely sketched out; but a threshold is crossed, the accumulation of detail suddenly effects a transformation of the whole, and a new form either appears or must be sought. The radical extension of data demands a new point of view for generalization. We come back to our question: Is there some new principle grasped here, some new point of departure for thought?

I think we may baptize it as *The Search for the Concrete*. We find this principle become most explicit precisely in the two philosophers who propose the most consciously revolutionary break with the whole philosophic tradition: Whitehead and Heidegger. Whitehead condemns two thousand years of philosophy (after Aristotle) for its mistaken notion of the concrete—for its "fallacy of misplaced concreteness." Heidegger remarks just as drastically: "Only by accomplishing the destruction of the ontological tradition do we obtain for the question of Being its true concreteness." Audacious words! We have abundant experience of the way tradition sneaks back to destroy its destroyers, but at least these men have formulated the principle on which they propose a revolutionary break, and it is worth our while to journey a little further into their uncharted land.

Where, how, does this movement begin? What insights, what questions, first launch it into the world? We have only succeeded so far in bringing this very complex tendency into momentary relief against the welter and fluidity of the schools of the past century; we have yet to define it as a really definite historical unit, with a more or less clearly marked point of inception, initial direction, and subsequent progress. The history of philosophy, when it is written at all, is written, not as a succession of opinions, but as a dialogue continuing in time. We have always taken this truth literally, and so we shall risk placing these two philosophies, of Whitehead and Heidegger, in a momentary exchange of dialectic. True, their philosophies develop in such radically different directions that they seem to agree only on the single point of orientation and the destructive role it is to play in relation to the whole philosophic tradition. But dialectic requires the tension of contrariety, and perhaps this dialogue, unfolding, will generate the dialectical theme that supplies the inner form of this historical movement. As an excuse for the liberty of making two other men speak for us, we might plead—with tongue very much in cheek, of course—the example of Aristotle's treatment of the pre-Socratic philosophers. He has often been accused of misrepresentation because he made them speak for him, but probably he would have retorted that what he was really interested in was exploring his own thought. This is what is known as the existential category of *appropriation*.

## An Imaginary Conversation

*Whitehead:* The occasion seems to demand something of a ritual. We are met to consummate the death of Descartes. It has taken him three centuries to die, and I do not think he is altogether dispatched yet. You, as the expert on death, ought to know what ritual is appropriate.

*Heidegger:* We ought to be sure, first, that we are really consummating the same death.

*W:* You mean, what do I wish to see interred? Very simply, the Cartesian dualism, which splits nature apart into the two incommensurable domains of matter and mind. But perhaps that does not tell the whole story. It begins with the "fallacy of misplaced concreteness."

*H:* The fallacy of what?

*W:* Misplaced concreteness. It is the fallacy of taking the abstract as concrete. Or, more precisely, of overlooking the degree of abstraction that may be involved in taking certain matters of fact as concrete. It is allied with another habit of thought, which I have baptized as "the fallacy of simple location."

*H:* Another one!

*W:* Well, the idea of this is already in Bergson. A body is present wherever it exercises an effect. To locate a body at a given point in space is a very complicated procedure, in the course of which the selected purposes and the degree of abstraction involved usually get forgotten.

*H:* I have expressed something like that in my notion of human *transcendence*. Human existence, *immediately and as such*, is in the world. A man's existence is not something that goes on inside his skin. He is always beyond himself.

*W:* Capital. Perhaps we shall even understand each other, who knows? But let us come back to our burial ritual. Now, Descartes did not invent this misplaced concreteness. Traditional philosophy, under the drug of Aristotle, had its doctrine of substance, according to which stones, trees, and tables were the ultimately concrete things in the world. Descartes simply carried this pernicious habit to its final impasse: he proceeded to isolate matter at the one pole of nature, and mind at the other. What he called matter was an abstract stuff in an abstract Euclidean space, and this highly abstract entity he took as an ultimate concrete, a substance. Consciousness did not fare any better at his hands: isolating a very rarefied self-consciousness, he left out of account all the concrete cluster of feelings, the unfailing "withness" of the body, which are ingredients in every conscious state. Naturally, after he had split nature into these two poles, he was bound to face the vexing question of how they could even be related to each other. This is the skeleton he leaves in the closet of modern philosophy. It leads to Hume's skepticism, and eventually to Kant's *Thing-in-itself*, forever inaccessible to human thought.

*H:* It certainly seems to me that I would move in your direction. I leave the physics to you, I would concentrate simply on the famous Cartesian truth, "I think, therefore I am." The trouble with this is that it puts the cart before the horse; on the contrary, we have to understand the "I am" before the "I think." Thinking is only a mode of human existence, after all. If we try to describe concretely the existence that thinks, we shall never be led to posit anything like Descartes's abstract subject as the thinker.

*W:* I hope we can continue to agree, but I cannot help

putting the question here: just what is the point of all this emphasis upon concreteness? Isn't it really the oldest question in philosophy itself, the question which the Ionian Greeks asked as soon as they raised their eyes toward their Mediterranean horizon, and began to wonder?

*H:* Yes and no. There was a sense to their question that they themselves did not grasp. Hegel has made *us* very conscious of it. Those ancient philosophers spoke of their principles as *archai*, points of beginning, and this aspect of their search is perhaps more significant than the abstractions of air, water, earth, and fire, in which they sought the underlying substance of all things. That is why Hegel makes so much of the question where to begin in philosophy. His answer is that you really may begin anywhere, because you are always beginning with the same thing, and it is the whole task of philosophy just to make this beginning explicit.

*W:* Let me try to come at it in another way. It is the old question of the whole and its parts, is it not, and the fact that the whole is more than the sum of its parts—

*H:* . . . that much abused catch phrase—

*W:* . . . which nevertheless conceals a profound truth. Hegel's point would be, would it not, that the concrete whole is already implicit in the parts that we seek to analyze?

*H:* Yes; when he analyzed your English empiricists for example, he showed that sense-data were intelligible only if we presupposed a concrete self-consciousness implicit in the act of sensing.

*W:* I learned that point from Bradley, and I have made my own use of it. But we are also touching upon Bergson's point about intuition, are we not? We cannot grasp a movement as a movement, for example, by adding up a set of positions. Unfortunately, Bergson simplified his point unduly, he contrasted intuition and intelligence as fixedly as if he were trying to erect another faculty psychology.

*H:* What happens often in the case of aesthetic experience would probably be the simplest and commonest illustration. I have seen a very intelligent man, a trained philosopher, trying to reason his way *into* the experience of a certain style that he was not able yet to appreciate. He asked himself, "What is experience? Sensation plus interpretation"—as if he could get inside that experience through a summation of parts. But no literary work was ever written by adding one sentence to another. If we are unable to live in the writer's world, we cannot explicate his single sentences formally.

*W:* Then we do not disagree about whole and part, that the parts themselves lose their sense away from their concrete whole—

*H:* Perhaps I would prefer to put it now in Kierkegaard's phrase, "the point of view," laying all the weight of emphasis upon this that he did. The question in understanding anything is whether we have the point of view or do not have it; whether we are really inside the point of view or on the outside.

*W:* Then, on the whole, it is really the same death we are consummating. I see you nod in agreement. Perhaps we should say that Descartes was a disaster if we did not remember the words of James Joyce (if an Englishman may quote an Irishman) that the errors of a genius are portals of discovery. Perhaps philosophy makes progress only by going to the end of blind alleys.

(We may pause here to observe that philosophers do not seem to be very different, after all, from you and me: they agree most when they are talking about the faults of other people. But, just as obviously as with you and me, this is not done out of malice: it is the only way they can define their own tasks historically. In this intermission, when the reader may draw breath and digest the argument so far, we may imagine that these two philosophers, who have almost certainly never read each other, are taking a rapid glance at each other's books. Now we cannot expect the agreement to last, when they go on to talk about themselves.)

*H:* It is time we came directly to the point. Where do you propose to find *your* concreteness?

*W:* I look for it in the deliverances of immediate perception, with all their richness and vagueness of content. "Perception" is not the adequate word here, but I use it in order to abbreviate what would be a very long description. Briefly, the concrete is the event. But every event, since it is a concrete fact of relatedness, is a kind of perceiving. The time of our perceptions is the specious present. This specious present is a block of duration, so to speak. Nature, in its aspect of becoming, is the emergent succession of such blocks of duration.

*H:* I should think on the contrary, that the more I surrender myself to the immediacy of perception, the more abstract it becomes. I am thinking precisely of the argument at the beginning of Hegel's *Phenomenology*.

*W:* Oh, but I have provided myself with a defense

against that Hegelian gambit. I do not talk at all about bare immediacy, and least of all the immediacy of a mere subject. I take the occasion of experience as an occasion within, indeed an occasion *of* the whole universe. The concrete is the whole universe in my specious present.

*H:* But Hegel's argument, all the same, may still work against you. Suppose we follow it concretely. You are fond of the English Romantic poets, and Wordsworth particularly, are you not?

*W:* I find that Wordsworth expresses well that fundamental fact which is the inflow of feelings from an enveloping nature. But why bring it up?

*H:* I will come to that question in a moment. Suppose, now, I walk in the green spring landscape with Wordsworth, and surrender myself, like him, to a "wise passiveness." To the inflow of feelings from an enveloping nature, as you just put it. I allow my perceptions to become soaked through, so to speak, with the greenness of the landscape. But the more I give myself to this immediacy the more I give myself to universals: greenness, blueness of sky, whiteness of cloud. In vain, you allege that I am here engaged with unique nuances of color, a unique nexus of quality. Whatever is a content of awareness can be repeated, and is therefore universal. Even that buzzing blooming tone of feeling that surrounds and permeates my perception is a conscious content, and as such can be repeated.

✗ No, it is I myself, my human reality, that is at the center of the scene and cannot be repeated. Relative to this human reality of mine, the specious present is a fragment that I am continually transcending, passing beyond, toward the future and the past. Immediate consciousness is a very paradoxical thing (and perhaps it does not even exist): it may contain material that I do not notice at all! The specious present represents a limiting condition to my attention, but only if I turn my attention in that direction: *viz.*, to the perception of small increments of change. Meanwhile, my consciousness is "elsewhere," in its future and past—and these specious presents (if they really do exist) ✗ flow by, beneath me, so to speak, unnoticed.

*W:* I remember now, I have heard this criticism before.

*H:* Perhaps I'm only making the same criticism that one of my cleverest followers has made against Bergson. Sartre maintains that Bergson is describing the flow of human consciousness as a natural phenomenon, seen from without, a thing in itself (*en soi*), budding and ripening before the observer's eye. But the point of view of human existence is not that it is in itself, but that it exists *for* itself, (*pour soi*). This cosmic emergence of events, no matter how delicately observed in its nuance and flux, does not in the least put us inside the human project. I should not have to remind you, an old Cambridge man, of all that old business about the specificity of the color yellow. We have another specificity here.

*W:* Well, the problem is, to put it logically, simply whether my descriptions can encompass all the data you bring forward. I think my notion of the person as a "superject" (rather than subject) can deal with what you say about the human project. (See, for example, my *Process and Reality*, p. 374.) But I suppose I am here principally as a "correlatee" and guest, to bring out your point of view rather than to take the platform for my own theories. Your point of view has become clearer to me; but I have just been wondering, in relation to what you have said, why it is you place such emphasis upon the pre-Socratic philosophers. Perhaps we may round off the matter if you explain what you see in those ancient philosophers.

*H:* That is a very good opportunity for me to make my point of view clearer. I think I can explain it more concisely than I have anywhere in my writings.

This dream of the pre-Socratics, the vision of their meaning, goes back to Nietzsche, who fell in love with the Greeks and the sunlight of their Mediterranean world. They were men, those Greeks, and recognized nothing higher in the universe than man himself, for even their gods were only men, a little larger, more powerful and passionate than the men we know. Nietzsche loved the pre-Socratic philosophers because they incarnated this overflowing sense of humanity. That man should really be the measure of all things, this was the highest flight of their wisdom, which Socrates distorted by giving it only the *banal* sense of pointing to a relativity of human mores, when in fact it brings forward its own absolute; an absolute which Nietzsche dared again to imagine with reverence and love.

Suppose we believe, really believe, that man is the highest existence in the universe. Do philosophers really grasp all that is implied in this—even those philosophers who philosophize, or pretend to philosophize, without any recourse to a deity? Have they gone to the depths of this belief, to see what forlornness, terror, and joy, lurk there? Do they understand what follows if there is nothing higher by which to explain human existence? If this existence has no other terms by which to interpret itself than its own: its projects, cares, death, and freedom? Bergson's flux of duration and your passage of events are only so much matter over which this human liberty takes its stand.

*W:* But how does Kierkegaard fit in with all this?

*H:* Of course he held that man exists in the end only by virtue of the absolute relation to the Absolute which is God. But notice how he deals with this. He does not, like the Catholic Thomist, plant this relation in man's being as a kind of natural tropism or gravitation toward God; on the contrary, it is the result of an absolute decision and a leap, founded upon the Absurd and the Paradox. Nietzsche could have made capital of this: the religious man *wills* that life shall have a meaning on the basis of what is possibly meaningless, an absurdity. Here is the Will to Power at its very apex. But when Kierkegaard repudiates Hegel, his point of view comes close to Nietzsche's. Having posited this Absolute Relation, Kierkegaard nevertheless insists that we must remain within one of its terms, human existence; that we cannot pretend, like Hegel, to penetrate into that other term, exploring the divine secrets by a rational dialectic. The "subjective thinker" seeks to explore human existence in its own terms because there is nothing higher that he *can* explore.

*W:* I am struck by the number of times that the name of Hegel has come up in this conversation.

*H:* He has been with us at almost every step, even where we may have been repudiating him. I mentioned that my argument against your immediate perception came straight out of his *Phenomenology.* True, Hegel's argument there has to do mainly with knowledge, while we have been talking directly about existence. But that in itself is a sign of how far we have progressed in the direction of concrete-

ness—something for which we have greatly to thank him.
Did you know, for example, that he discovered the "fallacy
of misplaced concreteness" long before you baptized it?

*W:* He *did!!*

*H:* It was an important stage of his dialectic to show that
the traditionally concrete objects of perception—stones,
trees, tables—are mere abstract fragments of existence.
Hegel aimed at somewhat the same revolution as yours and
mine: he upset the traditional contrast of abstract and concrete, universal and particular; gave the whole question a
new meaning and endowed it with a new dialectic. In fact,
we might say he began that search for the concrete, which
you in your direction, and I in a quite different one, have
tried to carry out.

*W:* And he too sought to consummate the death of Descartes?

*H:* Descartes and Kant too—

At which point we may conveniently ring down the curtain. Our dialogue has done its work: the dialectical theme
it developed has brought us closer to the center of the
movement we were describing and at the same time disclosed to us its source. There is no such thing as an absolute
beginning of any movement, much less of one so complex
as an historical movement of thought, and we could find
many predecessors of existentialism before Hegel. However, we have not been looking for historical anticipations
but something quite different: namely, the point at which a
principle implicit in a whole historical movement first became explicit and articulate. For present purposes, then, we
may rest with Hegel's *Phenomenology* as a beginning.

## Hegel and Kierkegaard

We are so familiar by this time with Kierkegaard's joke that Hegel walked out of existence into the System that we are likely to be a bit surprised when anybody locates the beginning of existentialism in Hegel. But rejection requires an antecedent kinship, and Kierkegaard could not have revolted if Hegel had not provided him with the weapons and, in part, the point of view for doing so.

Leaving aside the System with all its prestidigitations, let us try to catch some glimpse of Hegel at the very moment he faces existence itself. What was he thinking of when he protested against Kant as a particular representative of eighteenth-century rationalism?

"The trouble with Kant," the young and exuberant Hegel reflects, "is that he treats the thinking subject altogether too abstractly. He explores the human mind as if he were constructing an abstract geometry. This is his inheritance from Descartes, who thought he had got to the bottom of thinking when he arrived at the absolutely clear and distinct truth, 'I think'—a truth which had no reference to the quality, time, and place of the thinker. This 'I' who thinks—according to Descartes and Kant—is a completely abstract being, who does not exist at any particular time. But really! when I think, I am existing, and existence is inescapably historical. These categories themselves through which I attempt to grasp the world are the result of the long evolution of human experience, the deposit of the historical experience of mankind, and when I think, I am taking my place in this long chain of human thought, I am all mankind thinking at one stage of its history. (But perhaps I, Hegel, have gotten such hold of the truth, that the chain comes to an end in me, and mankind after me will simply have the task of filling in the details and interstices of the System.*)

"So, I have really grasped something concrete that was implicit in Kant's abstract geometry of the human consciousness, but that he himself did not see. Good God, what a genius I must have! What is this new principle? Simply this: that human consciousness is inexplicable except in terms of a concrete developing Self, which evolves by making its differences explicit and then attempting to unify them in a larger whole. Otherwise all that business of the Kantian schemata and categories is a skeleton without either an accompanying physiology or an evolutionary biology that would make the anatomy intelligible. Lo, the vision is upon me, the veil of the future is rent, and I see in the next century a philosopher named Whitehead (who will know a new kind of physics) proclaiming that Kant's categorical scheme actually occurs within the framework of Newtonian physics, and thus merely represents human thinking at one historical stage."

We may leave Hegel at this moment of his vision—somewhere shortly after *l'an trentiesme de son age*. Was Kierkegaard justified, then, in accusing him of walking out of existence into the System? I think he was, for Hegel had no sooner walked into an existential point of view than he continued on out of it—like a man who gets stuck in a revolving door, for a moment is really inside the building, then

---

* *Sotto voce*, the Unconscious speaking around 1807. Later, in the 1830's the old man, drunk with his vision, really believed it.

continues the original push around, and is back in the bleak out-of-doors again. What happened?

Simply this: from the perception of human thinking as existential, Hegel took another step—which we may call the Hegelian leap—to the conclusion that existence itself was rational and therefore could be put inside logic. "My thought," Hegel reasoned, "not only represents humanity thinking at one particular stage in its history, but this consciousness has also come to be within the whole context of nature, and is in fact the whole universe become conscious in me. Unless this consciousness is a curious kind of sport with no real relation to the universe in which it appears (the possibility that haunts Kant's thinking), then the universe itself must be thoroughly accessible to human thinking. If my thought is to count for anything, then it must make sense of this universe, and nothing less than the whole universe. And that requires that the Whole itself be rational." At which point Hegel burst into a loud hosanna, and began to build the System.

When I think, then, not only history but the whole of Nature and the Absolute are incarnated in my thought and when we read Hegel, we are really supposed to have been moving all along through God's mind itself! Perhaps Hegel was only a madman who thought he was Hegel. But like most madmen, he had abundant reasons for what he was doing. The Hegelian leap, we have seen, was the outcome of two separate principles: 1) the positing of the concrete developing Self to explain thinking, and 2) the intellectual demand of intelligibility. But in Hegel's treatment this second principle breaks down into two aspects: he demanded not only that the universe be intelligible in its totality, for which he needed to posit an Absolute, but also that it be intelligible to him, Hegel—at which point he leaped into the Absolute's mind and declared himself privy to its secrets. There is in all this one of the great unconscious ironies of history, for Hegel, who thought he was really bringing the rationalism of the Enlightenment to its completion, actually created instead a new cabala, in which all things were turned into signs, cryptic and interrelated, of the divine presence.

But while the Absolute continued its march through history, Hegel the man, marching to his classroom, lost his shoe on the road. Here Kierkegaard, "the spy," observes and objects. God has numbered the hairs of our head, the Gospel tells us, and apart from the divine intentions not a sparrow (not even Hegel's shoe) falls to the ground. That is all very true, but for God not for Hegel, and it is hardly to be taken seriously that Hegel, an existing man and professing Christian, should pretend to be in on the divine intentions. There is a gulf between finite and infinite, God and his creatures, that cannot be made to disappear by dialectical manipulation and approximation. Otherwise, what is the point of Christianity at all? The Hegelian System really dispenses with the whole point of Christianity. For what precisely does Christianity teach but that I, a concrete being existing in despair and uneasiness, need a Redeemer to appear in history in order to save me? This is a symbol of the gulf between God and His creatures—a gulf that was bridged only by the Scandal and the Paradox, the appearance of Christianity in history—and a sign therefore that no existing man can hope to plant himself within the divine Mind and think Its thoughts for It. Since Hegel had his

Dialectic, he hardly needed Jesus Christ in order to be saved.

Passing over the issue of Christianity, we can isolate from Kierkegaard's attack the simple point of human *truthfulness*, the will to remain faithful to human experience itself. Reading Hegel, we are always divided between admiration for his genius and shock, even disgust, at a certain coarseness of mind by which he can override the rough edges of contingency, chance, human existence itself. Hegel has the histrionic ability necessary to any genius, he dared the Grand Style and carried it off with success; but he is a little too much the actor locked tightly in the armor of his solemnity, unable to relax and regard himself at any point with irony. Consider his treatment of the "unhappy consciousness," which may be taken as Kierkegaard himself, and the place Hegel assigns to it in his dialectic is the place he would assign to the unhappy Dane. This unhappy consciousness—divided and alienated from itself—is merely one stage, and an early one, in the Dialectic of Reason. That is, our human suffering is really the result of an incomplete rationalism. The unhappy consciousness disappears in a higher synthesis with the knowledge that we are not cut off from the universe; disappears as soon as consciousness knows itself to be identical with the whole of Reality, and Reality itself to be rational. Here Kierkegaard's objection becomes a positive revolt. How can my suffering—the despair of my own unique existence—be made to disappear by being enclosed in a logical system? Suppose the universe is a logical system, how does that lighten my suffering—which is an absolute for me—make it more bearable, give it meaning? Christianity is more honest than Hegel (and whether Christians or not, we must agree with Kierkegaard here), for it professes to lighten my suffering by offering me an eternal happiness in return for my renunciation on this earth.

This is the historical explanation of Hegel: the exuberance of early German Romanticism sublimating itself in the confident rationalism of the Enlightenment. Now, it is just these two tendencies that supply the opposed tensions which eventually split the System apart. Hegel, seeking to put existence into logic, is like a man who plants an acorn in a flower pot; the plant grows and splits the vase, and Kierkegaard is there to harvest what Hegel had planted. *In Kierkegaard, the Underground Man acquires his philosophic voice.* This does not mean that the resentment, spite, and aching liver of Dostoevsky's creature appear in the gentle, beautiful soul of the Dane. Those were qualities that Dostoevsky needed in order to define his character fictionally, and particularly to give him a place in relation to the Russian society of the 1870's. The philosophic significance of the Underground Man, going beyond this social reference, is just that he proclaims his own existence a surd that cannot be resolved without remainder into any purely logical structure, and it is this that Kierkegaard brings to explicit philosophic expression.

With this, existentialism acquires both its name and its birth, and our brief account of its genesis may come to an end. Yet it is significant that, while Kierkegaard's works were buried in obscurity until the beginning of this century, nevertheless other philosophers during the last part of the nineteenth century went along their own existential paths, carrying out their own revolts against Hegel, Idealism, or Classical Rationalism. The epoch itself had spread its tentacles into the minds of its philosophers; far from being the work of one special school, the existential movement represents a true tendency of the whole historical period, in which we too still exist.

# II

## Existentialism Seeks Its System

THERE MIGHT SEEM to be some sort of contradiction in this title, as if Hegel were returning to enjoy a kind of revenge against Kierkegaard. But existential philosophers could not continue to communicate fragments. Every meaning, however fragmentary, seeks a system; it was one of Hegel's great contributions to have understood this so thoroughly, and in fact Kierkegaard could communicate successfully by his indirect method, by scraps and fragments, chiefly against the background of the Hegelian system, which was already in existence and widely known.

But we need hardly raise any abstruse questions of system, for we wish simply to turn now from our account of the genesis of Existentialism to consider its principal themes. And if we choose Heidegger as our subject, the reason is one of pure convenience, for he has gathered together the leading threads of Kierkegaard, Nietzsche, Dilthey, and others, and woven them into a more unified pattern. I do not mean to imply in the least that Heidegger is the most important of the philosophers with whom we have had to deal here, but he does strike me as the most self-conscious in his attempt to place himself in relation to the whole tradition of Western thought, and this consciousness of tradition does in itself supply us with so many handles or keys by which we may appropriate his meaning. Heidegger, moreover, has been the principal point of departure for the French existentialists, particularly those of Sartre's school, and their contributions beyond him have so far largely been certain new emphases, details of further explication, and the eloquence of individual temperament. At this point, then, we propose nothing more than a job of straightforward exposition, which may serve to make accessible to the English reader the main outlines of Heidegger's thought.

But this is not at all the simple job it sounds, for the whole structure of Heidegger's thought seems to nestle so closely in the bosom of the German language that all his writing might be alleged as evidence for an inescapable identification of thought and language. Probably these difficulties of language banish to a remote future, if we shall ever see it at all, the time when Heidegger's writing, in any considerable bulk, will be available in English translation; which possibility would seem to supply an additional point and usefulness to any effort of simple exposition now. We shall confine ourselves principally to his chief work, *Being and Time* (1927), which, besides being by far the best of his books, setting a standard to which he never came near again, is also the most comprehensive, containing all the themes that he was to elaborate or modulate (not always fortunately, alas) in his subsequent writings. By reason of its completeness, we may take it as being something of a Bible of non-religious existentialism—or if this seems a bit paradoxical, anyway a very convenient textbook.

## Being and Time

Heidegger proposes for himself the goal of elucidating the meaning of Being, *in general*—Being, as it is everywhere and in all things. If the proposal does not look very promising at first view, nor very novel, nevertheless the means of his investigation do attract us, for he seeks to discover the meaning of Being from the analysis and description of human being. In fact, all that we have of the *Being and Time* is this preparatory analysis of human being; the second part —in which he was to deal, after this lengthy preparation, with the question of Being in general—Heidegger has never published, perhaps with good reason, as I shall later suggest.

The trouble with all previous metaphysics, Heidegger says, is that it attempted to understand human being from the categories of Nature. This tradition took its point of departure from Aristotle's *Metaphysics*, and the medieval Schoolmen simply perfected logically most of Aristotle's points. (In the process they may also have lost certain of the meanings, the overtones, that Heidegger is struggling to restore to philosophy; a point very much worth exploring —but we simply mention it here, and pass on.) This tradition from Aristotle through the Schoolmen even dominates the idealist Hegel, at least in his most "metaphysical" work, his *Logic*. Now, in contrast to this long tradition, Heidegger proposes something analogous to what Kant called a Copernican Revolution in philosophy: he intends to understand Being, in general, from the fact of human being.

But the point of departure of his Copernican Revolution is very different from that of Kant. Kant, he says, was too much under the spell of Descartes, and Heidegger wishes to place himself in revolt also against the three centuries of Western philosophy initiated by Descartes. Descartes made the proposition *Cogito, ergo sum* (I think, therefore I am) basic to his philosophizing, arriving at the fact that *I am* from the fact of thinking. Kant, following him, located a pure or Transcendental Ego (the *I* in the "I think" after Descartes's reduction) as the ultimate subject of all experience. This is wrong, says Heidegger, we must invert this order: we must understand the *Cogito* from the *Sum;* unless we understand man's being we cannot understand his thoughts (*cogitationes*) or his thinking.

(Admirable. But then we immediately wonder how close this brings Heidegger again to the other tradition from which he is in revolt—the tradition of Aristotle and the Schoolmen, who also began with Being rather than Thought. Heidegger's revolt against two long traditions in philosophy places him in a new and unique relation of balance or tension between these traditions. The question then becomes: How stable is this balance? We shall come back to this later.)

Why should man be given this precedence over other beings in nature as a starting point for the new metaphysics (or ontology) that Heidegger proposes? Because, says Heidegger, man is the metaphysical (or ontological) animal: in being he is concerned with his own being. Man seeks to understand his own being, and this search itself is a fact that characterizes profoundly his being. And when he poses the problem of Being, in general, he ought to begin from this being who is concerned about his own being, if that study is to achieve a new concreteness.

In his description of human existence, Heidegger resolutely avoids the use of the terms "man," "human," "human being," which might carry traditional connotations of a definite human nature. Instead he uses the word *"Dasein,"* a common German philosophical term to designate *existence,* which in his use is also meant to preserve its literal meaning of "being-there" (*sein-da*). Man, for Heidegger, is Mr. Being There. I.e., man always exists in a situation, he comes to consciousness of himself in a world, surrounded by factual conditions which he himself has not created.

The reason for this choice of terminology lies, in great part, in Heidegger's historical derivation from the great German philosopher Wilhelm Dilthey. Heidegger indicates his historical relation to Dilthey at several places, but perhaps too briefly for its full depth and breadth to be seen by the unprepared reader. But without Dilthey's researches, the daring of *Being and Time* as an interpretation of human existence could never have been projected by Heidegger.

Dilthey's contribution to the history of thought can be best outlined perhaps in terms of his departure from Hegel's brand of historical thinking. Hegel sought to incorporate the whole of history within the compass of reason. He sought to put history inside mind. Dilthey started from a more or less Hegelian historicism, but soon worked away from it. He (like Marx) also turns Hegel on his head: Dilthey seeks to locate mind in history. His historical researches led him to see the various philosophical systems of the past as historical configurations existing in relation to their historical period, to the cultural and social context of their epoch. The fundamental category for Dilthey became that of *life*, and all philosophical systems were to be interpreted as offshoots of man's total life as lived through the framework of his cultural and social conditions. Mind must be construed in relation to this category of life. *Man*, according to Dilthey, *does not have a nature but only a history*. Human nature is plastic; human life differs strikingly, in its characteristics and presuppositions, in different times and places: classical man differs from medieval man differs from Renaissance man differs from modern man.

But Dilthey's shortcoming, Heidegger says, was that, having arrived at this great generalizing idea of Life, he did not analyze its structure. Heidegger attempts to make up for this shortcoming not by analyzing the concept of Life, which would fall under the special science of biology, but by analyzing the structures of human existence itself. Man's existence, says Heidegger, is prior to his essence; or, more exactly, man's existence is his essence. It is easy to see how this comes out of Dilthey's proposition that man does not have a nature but only a history. Heidegger has only taken one step beyond Dilthey; the radical daring of his interpretation takes off from the prior conclusions at which Dilthey arrived. What Heidegger means is that it is human existence itself, facing its tasks, transcending its past and projecting itself toward its future, that transforms and recreates the structures, social and factual, surrounding it, and which philosophers hitherto have too easily taken as being human nature itself.

## Human Existence: Primary Features of Description

The first thing to notice is that existence is never just
existence in general. On the contrary, existence is always
mine, yours, his, etc.—that is, it is always personal. This
does not mean that Heidegger is going to interpret his
existence by seeking out a pure *I*—a pure or transcendental
Ego—as the subject of all experience. On the contrary,
Heidegger locates existence, immediately and at the first
stroke, in the public world and among other people. Here
he gives phenomenology a radical shift in point of departure
from that of Husserl,* who had entered into the phenomenological domain of the given by isolating, in the manner of
Kant, a pure Ego involved in all consciousness. In com-

---

* Edmund Husserl (1859–1938) had been a mathematician before
entering the field of philosophy. His first book, *Philosophy of Arithmetic* (1891), combines both these interests, attempting to explore the
sources of our basic notions of number.

In *Logical Investigations* (1900–01) he began his attack upon the
"psychologism" of the period. The reigning ideas in psychology had
been largely inherited from British empiricism via the psychologist
Wundt, who had established the first experimental psychological labo-
ratory in the 1870's. The mental life was supposed to consist of elementary ideas or experiences, combined by the laws of association into
more complex ones, analogous to the way in which in physics atoms
cluster together into molecules of greater and greater complexity. For
Husserl, these preconceptions were entirely inadmissible: the life of
consciousness could not be construed in terms of atoms of ideas
bumping into each other and coagulating according to certain com-
binatory laws; the realm of mind was one of intentions and meanings,
not of forces and causes (understood always by some secret analogy
with physics).

These dissatisfactions with "psychologism" eventually led Husserl
to develop his own idea of phenomenology, the complete scope of
which he outlined in *Ideas* (1913). Phenomenology, in his view, would
attempt a systematic description of the data of consciousness without
making any preconceptions about those data—whether these precon-

parison with this "subjective" approach, Heidegger's is radically "objective." (How far it takes him from the tradition of German philosophy, I do not believe he himself is fully conscious, despite his various pronunciations about the revolutionary and tradition-destroying nature of his approach—another point of tension within his system, to which we shall return later.) Heidegger proposes to understand our human existence by beginning from our ordinary everyday existence (banality, *Altäglichkeit*), rather than from the purified philosophical existence that is reached after we practice the Cartesian doubt about the existence of external objects and other people—and this everyday existence is always *in* the world and *with* others. To be means to be *in* the world and to be *with* others. *Dasein* is always

---

ceptions came from previous theory or traditional and lazy habits of language. Experience, which is a palimpsest scribbled over by inherited slogans and empty formulae, was to be wiped clean. This was to be a new beginning for philosophy. For, in getting to the sources of experience, beyond all preconceptions, philosophy would attain a new rigor.

Husserl conceived that this discipline would require the long and careful collaboration of many minds, and he gathered a number of disciples around him. Occupying the chair of philosophy at Freiburg, he had become by this time the most influential philosopher in Germany. In the 1920's he launched a series of *Yearbooks for Phenomenological Research*, which published a number of important works, among them Heidegger's *Being and Time*.

Though Heidegger considered himself at the time to be a respectful disciple, his book was not received with satisfaction by the master. Indeed, the ultimate aims, as well as the starting points, of the two men are vastly different. Husserl chose to stay resolutely within the standpoint of consciousness, and so remained, fundamentally, a Cartesian. As late as 1931, in his *Cartesian Meditations*, he still presented phenomenology as a refinement upon the thought of Descartes. Heidegger, on the contrary, has always understood his own philosophy as an attempt to overcome Descartes and the whole legacy of Cartesianism that lurks within modern culture.

*da-sein,* i.e. is always *there* (*da*), in a situation, and is always Being-with (*Mitsein*) others.

But what is the subject of this everyday existence? *Who* is it we are really speaking of now as being in the world and with others?

It is not, Heidegger tells us, the pure I that philosophers have isolated as the subject of all experiences. It is a much more common and humble creature. Heidegger calls this creature of everyday existence the One (*das Man*). Who is this One? Everybody and Nobody. He is the one we refer to in all the prescriptions of public behavior: "One does this, one doesn't do that, one doesn't smoke here, etc." This One is, so to speak, the mere point of intersection of all these prescriptions of the public and external behavior of every-day existence. Thus, Everybody and Nobody.

It is significant that we locate this subject of everyday existence—this existence who is in the world and with others—through the clues of *language.* Heidegger's brief and passing remarks upon language make up one of the most pregnant of his analyses in *Being and Time;* they contain many fruitful hints for literary critics, and he himself has carried them into the domain of criticism in his discussions of the German poet Hölderlin; and these views of language have become fundamental to much of the criticism now being practiced in France. Language, according to Heidegger, is speech, and speech is always given along with our world and other people. Our everyday existence *is* in speech. Our Being-in-the-world comes to expression in speech, and through expression to interpretation and understanding. Thus, speech is not primarily a means of expressing interior psychic states of a pure inner consciousness.

On the contrary, speech is through and through "worldly," belonging to and including the world. Robinson Crusoe on his island was not outside of language: he existed still in relation to others and to language; it happened only that the mode of this relation was the mode of absence and the mode of silence.

But in everyday life the speech through which the One expresses itself is *chatter*. *Chatter* and *ambiguity*—these are the characteristics of the everyday Being-in-the-world. They characterize, with respect to One's language, the *fallen* state of the One that we all are, so far as we are in the banal public everyday world. This state of Fall (*Verfallen*) which Heidegger describes, has nothing to do with the fall from grace of which theologians treat—though, as a matter of historical fact, some of its principal descriptive features are derived from the descriptions theology has given. Nor does it entail in any way a lower degree of reality, in the manner of some traditional metaphysical systems. On the contrary, it is just as real, Heidegger stresses, as the *authentic* human existence that manages to escape from it. Heidegger even says that it is not a value judgment that separates this state of Fall from that of authentic human existence (which latter we shall describe in a moment)—though we can hardly subscribe to this statement since it is he *as a value-seeker* who is led to make these different descriptions of the two possibilities of human existence.

What are the full characteristics of this fallen state of everyday existence? They have to be seen from another point of view: everyday existence—no matter how public and banal—is always pierced and permeated by some feeling, some affective state (*Befindlichkeit*). To exist is to be

in some mood or other: fear, anxiety, tranquility, or joy.
Feeling is a fundamental mode of existence. The world is
given to us in feeling. Heidegger is not talking of feeling
as a modification of an inner consciousness which is then
*projected* onto things outside, and so "colors" the world
given to us at any moment. That is a state of affairs already
cut up by analysis and therefore much more sophisticated
than the primary unity of world and feeling—given together—that is our concrete reality in daily life.

Anxiety (*Angst*) is the fundamental feeling precisely
because it is directed toward the whole world more plainly
than any other feeling. Anxiety is indefinite: it is not about
this or that object, we are simply anxious and we do not
know about what; and when it is over, we have to say that
"it was about nothing."* This is what the psychoanalysts
call free-floating anxiety; anxiety without any discoverable
object. Of course, the psychoanalysts are able to discover
in the case of certain patients the very definite causes and
circumstances that engender this anxiety. But the empirical
discovery of its genesis does not do away with Heidegger's
point since he is concerned not with the genesis but the
content of the state: namely, in what manner we are existing when we exist in that state. What we are anxious
about in such states, Heidegger tells us, is our very Being-
in-the-world as such. That is why anxiety is more fundamental to human existence than fear. Fear is always definite; about this or that object in the world; but anxiety is
directed toward our Being-in-the-world itself, with which

---

* Unfortunately, Heidegger plays badly with this manner of speech
in his essay, *What is Metaphysics?* But in *Being and Time* he avoids
this particular word-play.

every definite object, or thing, within the world is involved. Thus anxiety, more than any other feeling, discovers to us the world: i.e., brings us face to face with a world, to which we now sense ourselves to be in precarious relation. Anxiety, like speech, is through and through "worldly"—belonging to and revealing the world.

Anxiety thus gives us the first clue to an authentic existence possible for the human person. But in ordinary life we usually evade the condition: we try to transform this indefinite anxiety into a definite fear or worry about this or that particular object. Thus authentic anxiety disappears, in our banal existence, into curiosity and inquisitiveness (*Neugier*). Here Heidegger is borrowing from the Christian tradition, which represented the worldly existence of man (as opposed to a genuine religious existence) as one of dispersion (*dispersio*)—a state in which man perpetually busies himself with diversions and distractions from himself and his own existence: "distracted from distraction by distraction."

But this fallen state is not one of complete worthlessness. Analyzing it, we have already gone a good distance in discovering the essential characteristics of man's existence. Moreover, if the human being is able to become really a Self —to discover and achieve an authentic mode of existence— it will not involve his retreating from all the modes of everyday existence. In fact, such a retreat would be impossible; we must all—even the authentic self, provided we are able to achieve such—exist in the world with others, speaking, busying ourselves with cares about this or that particular object. Authenticity is only a question of a modification, slight but profound, within our everyday existence, which places this existence in a new and altogether different perspective.

Heidegger is here drawing upon Kierkegaard's notion of Repetition: the man who really arrives at the religious stage of existence, says Kierkegaard, makes the absolute renunciation of worldly existence, but he expects that it will all be restored to him. Job renounces before God and then all his worldly goods are restored. So the Knight of Faith, says Kierkegaard, comes back cheerfully to ordinary humdrum existence, which becomes much richer and more satisfying than for the Knight of Despair, who, because he has not yet gone beyond it through the absolute renunciation, is not able to come back to it for what it is. For Heidegger too, the question of an authentic human existence involves this "small piece of spice that will season the whole dish"—that slight modification that will take us out of everyday existence, but then restore it to us fully for what it is. To be sure, Heidegger is not going to find this possibility of an authentic existence in any kind of religious leap. Quite the contrary.

## Care

Having elucidated various aspects of the human condition as it shows itself in everyday life, can we now gather together all these threads into one pattern, under one unifying concept? Yes, says Heidegger, and this unifying concept for the human condition is *Care*. Care expresses the whole nature of our being insofar as we exist in the world and with others.

This essential trait of Care, which permeates our human existence, is revealed to us in the primary feeling of anxiety.

Anxiety flows from the fundamental trait of man: that *he is a being whose being is characterized by the fact that he is concerned about his own being.* This separates him from all other beings in the universe, and Care is simply the concretion of this quality in our everyday existence. Even the mode of our Being-in-the-world points to this primary aspect of Care. We are not in the world as an object in a box; not in a sense of occupying a given point or points in an abstract and geometrical space—that is a much later notion developed by the abstractive operations of science; no, the primary sense (i.e., the sense that is *given* to us directly in our everyday life) is that we are in the world in that we *take care* for this or that object among the objects surrounding us. The notion of a world in which we exist is discovered to us through the immediate environment of objects in which we move, which we take care of, are apprehensive and concerned about, attend to. Care expresses the fundamental character of experience as we move through the world about the tasks of everyday existence.

Heidegger quotes, as a kind of literary summation of his phenomenological analysis, a beautiful Latin fable that Goethe, learning of it from Herder, drew upon for the second part of his *Faust* (the most philosophical of all his poems):

One day when Care was crossing a river, she saw some clay on the bank. She took up a piece and began to fashion it. While she was still reflecting over what she had made, Jupiter arrived on the scene. Care asked him to give the shape a spirit or soul, which Jupiter promptly did. Then a dispute arose between them: each wanted to give his own name to the new creation. While they were disputing, Earth came up and insisted that her name be given to the new creature, since she had furnished it with its body. The three of them called in Saturn to judge the dispute. "Jupiter," said Saturn, "since you have given the thing a soul, you shall receive this after its death; you, Earth, shall finally receive the body; but since Care first shaped this creature, she shall possess it as long as it lives. As for the quarrel over the creature's name—let him be called Man (*homo*) since he is fashioned of earth (*humo*).

Man, as long as he is in the world, is to be possessed by Care. The fable illustrates Heidegger's meaning only in that one point, for his whole analysis dispenses with any reference to a possible immortality: there is no soul which is received in Jupiter's or Abraham's bosom after death. Moreover, when earth finally gets the body, the possibilities that constitute human existence have been canceled, and it is no longer a man but a *thing*. Remove the dualism of the fable (the whole of Heidegger's analysis is directed against any dualism between soul and body) and you get the fundamental point: Care is the being of man.

## Death

But since Care is always pointed at the absent and the future, it seems to give human existence a singular incompleteness and make it impossible to grasp this existence as a whole and integral structure. It is to this task that Heidegger addresses himself now in his analysis of *death*, for any attempt to grasp our existence as a whole must send us toward the fact of death, which concludes that existence.

His analysis of death is perhaps the most important and satisfying interpretation in his whole picture of man. It is, in a certain way, the keystone of his analysis, since we are able to attain an authentic existence only if we come face to face unblinkingly with the possibility of our death, for it is death that tears us out of the external banality of everyday existence. What, then, are the main points in a phenomenology of death?

*First:* It is impossible to experience the death of others. No matter how much I may suffer, sympathetically, their actual death-pangs, no matter how much I may be afflicted personally by the loss of the person deceased, the fact remains that it is his death and not mine, and the very meaning of death is that it robs me of my own being. Just as no one else can relieve me of my death by taking it upon himself, so it is impossible for me to experience death as a fact happening to someone else. Death is not a public fact occurring out there in the world: it is something that happens within my own human existence.

*Second:* Death is not the end of human life in the sense in which the end of a road may be the termination of a journey. When I arrive at the end of my journey, I still exist, and existing, I am in the state of having completed something. But when death comes, I no longer exist and so there is no journey which, properly speaking, I can be said to have completed. ("What has been concluded, that *I* can have concluded it"—to paraphrase William James's moving deathbed statement.) Moreover, when I am halfway along the journey, I can be at its termination only by crossing the remaining half of the road; but death is an end of human life in the sense that it may cut short my existence at any moment. "As soon as we are born we are old enough to die," Heidegger quotes the proverb. The life that is allotted me is not a well-laid-out road at the end of which is death, but death *as a possibility* permeates my existence from the moment I am thrown into this world I never made.

Having made these two negative points, how then are we to conceive, concretely and positively, of death in its relation to our human existence? To answer this, Heidegger turns to the analysis of everyday existence and asks how death appears in that context.

Our everyday existence is dominated by the One, the external public individual. The One has some very cute tricks to play in order to escape the prospect of death. First, we— insofar as we are this One of banal life—transform death into a *fact*, an occurrence within the world along with other events. We read about deaths (as so many facts) in the obituary columns of newspapers. We attend funerals as public and social occasions, regulated by their own complex prescriptions as to how *one* is to behave there. All the rites and ceremonies surrounding death aim at transforming it into a public event. By this means the One very cunningly tries to fob off death as something that happens to Everybody, and therefore precisely to Nobody—neither to me, you, nor any real self.

In a story by Tolstoy, "Ivan Ilyich," the hero lies on his deathbed facing for the first time the prospect of *his own* death; long ago he had read in his school logic text the example of a syllogism, "All men are mortal, Caius is a man, therefore Caius is mortal." Precisely—Caius was mortal, but who was this Caius? Caius was not he, Ivan Ilyich, who had had that childhood, those parents, this particular life. It was all right for Caius to be mortal (for Caius is the One, and therefore, Nobody in particular); but that he, poor Ivan

Ilyich, should be mortal, should face death!—that is the shattering and inexplicable prospect he now faces. Everything in Heidegger's analysis of death is implicit in Tolstoy's story; Heidegger has simply placed Tolstoy's perceptions within the framework of a more or less rigorous phenomenology.

The One has another clever trick too: not only does it make out death as something that happens to other people, but also as something that will occur at another and later time. In our banal chatter, we say, "To be sure, death comes to all," but we tacitly understand: "But it does not come *now*, we have plenty of time ahead of us." We keep thinking of death as the end of a journey, and comfortably imagine that a great part of the road stretches still in front of us. Death, however, is not a fact but a possibility. And its real character as a possibility is that *it is possible at any moment*. "As soon as a man is born he is old enough to die."

But notice an even more significant point in the everyday attitude toward death. Despite the fact that it flees from the consciousness of death, our everyday existence reveals itself as essentially pointed toward death. We exist continuously in relation to death, it happens only that the manner of this relation, as it appears in daily life, is essentially Being-toward-death. Death, as the end of existence (in the authentic sense of end), is present in human existence from the beginning.

But death—once truly grasped as this possibility—also affords us the first glimpse of a possible *authentic* existence for man. Confronting death as possible at any moment, we are torn out of the context of banal life, and restored to a Self, which must face death without disguise. This was the experience of Ivan Ilyich on his deathbed. Authenticity means no more than to become oneself truly through the *Resoluteness* (*Entschlossenheit*) with which we face death. Death is liberating: it frees us from the servitude of petty cares that threaten to engulf ordinary existence completely, and delivers us to the essential *projects* by which we make our own existence. Popular language almost recognizes this, saying, "Life is too short to worry about those (petty) things." This is in the right direction, though the language still betrays the deception of the One, referring to the future as a *thing* that is there, ahead of us, waiting till we travel the road to it. Better to say, in more authentic language, "I shall die, and what does anything matter beside my becoming the Self that I must become." And even joyfully: "Thank God, there is death, for how should I live otherwise? I might go on indefinitely being someone else, someone unconsciously false."

This is the human condition that Heidegger calls *Freedom-toward-death*. Suspended over death, "over seventy fathoms," moving at every moment within this perpetual possibility of nothingness, which is the authenticity of death, we are also released at last into an authentic human freedom. The chain has slipped away, and whatever movement, whatever project, we launch against the background of this void, has nothing to rest upon but ourselves, and just in this do we know ourselves to be free. But this authentic freedom, which is disclosed to us as we confront death, represents only the completion, the full realization, of the freedom which in fact lies at the very source of existence. This freedom is presupposed in Heidegger's system from the very beginning, since, banishing the notion of a fixed human nature, he has defined man's existence as his essence—as that which creates his essence. The doctrine of human freedom is essential to any existentialism.

Perhaps we are indebted to Sartre, even more than Heidegger, for emphasizing freedom and placing it at the center of his thought. Heidegger does not attempt any elaborate philosophic arguments to demonstrate that the freedom of the will is a fact; he presupposes, rather, that freedom is part of the phenomenologically given—something that is immediately grasped as soon as we grasp that man is to be defined by his possibilities. Sartre, however, has attempted a more thoroughgoing phenomenological validation of this freedom, which, if not precisely a demonstration, may be taken to fill, in his thought, the place of the traditional arguments in favor of freedom of the will.

Freedom requires otherness and negation, and man, says Sartre, brings negation with him into the universe. Conscious Being (*l'etre-pour soi*) is defined by the characteristic that it violates the Law of Identity: man is not what he is at any given moment, and he is what he is not, for he is his future which is not yet, and his past which is no longer. Thus the yawning gap of negation appears within the dense plenitude of Being, and out of this gap arises human possibility and human freedom. Man is free, Sartre is saying, because he can always say no to what exists. Orestes, confronting Jupiter, can always say no—even to the omnipotence which can crush him; so too, the French Resistance can always say no to the occupying Germans, however near they be to military and political omnipotence.

But is this resolute confrontation of death possible in fact as well as merely in principle? Heidegger finds the indication of this real possibility in the voice of *conscience*. But in the experience of conscience, who cries; and to whom, and what does it cry? We cry to ourselves; but the self that cries is not something that already exists, but something that *is to be*—i.e., is projected as future. This is the basis on which Heidegger finds man's being permeated by the negative, by nothingness. That on which we seek to ground ourself— justify ourself—is *not yet*: a self that we seek to bring into being. And we exist as men not by relapsing back into being what we are—like a thing, a stone or table—but to the extent to which our whole being is projected toward that which does not yet exist, which is to be, but is never realized and possessed in its completeness like a thing. However negative this language, it is really at the opposite pole from nihilism. When Heidegger says (with James Joyce) that man's being is founded on the void, he intends this as an affirmation of human life—in the only sense in which it can be an *authentically* human life. Modern man has been haunted by the smell of death and nothingness now for over a century; here Heidegger follows Nietzsche by affirming life but not stopping his nostrils.

## Time

All the foregoing analysis has been only to clear the ground for the interpretation of time as the very *meaning* of existence. It should already be evident from the analysis of Care that man's being is temporal through and through. This temporal character of human existence Heidegger calls *temporality* (*Zeitlichkeit*), and it is to be distinguished from the "vulgar" conception of *time* (*Zeit*), which is an affair of clocks, chronometers, and calendars, encountered within the world of man's care.

Since man's nature is Care, his being is to be projected always toward a future. Man must be defined by his possibilities: "Man is always infinitely more than what he is at any given moment." The *future* reveals itself as that toward which existence is projected; the *past* as that which our existence perpetually transcends—i.e., goes beyond, or rises above—and toward which also we may turn back in choosing to affirm this or that part of the past; the *present* is that in which we make-present, realize, a future in this transcending of the past. Future, past, and present are thus given to us together as defining an inescapably temporal existence. Heidegger calls them the three *ecstasies* of temporality. The word "ecstasy" here retains the meaning of the Greek original, *ekstasis:* displacement. Future, present, past are three aspects into which our existence is horizontally displaced, and here again man's existence appears essentially incomplete, perpetually displaced or spread out into these three phases.

Notice that Heidegger does not conceive of this primary temporality as a time-series—a series of instants sliding from future through present into the past. This "vulgar" notion of the time-series as the primary datum of our temporal existence results fundamentally from the unauthentic existence of everyday life, where time appears as something that passes moment by moment. If we have not resolutely taken our existence into our own hands, and projected it, in full anticipation of our death, toward the future, then life must appear only as a series of moments that passively succeed each other. Only on the level of an authentic existence do we glimpse the more basic meaning of future, present, past as three "ecstasies" of existence.

But Heidegger also affirms, against philosophers like Bergson, that this "vulgar" concept of time as a series—something measured by clocks and calendars—has its valid place within the phenomenological structure. It is a valid aspect of our Being-in-the-world, a valid part of that world which is the object of our prudent carefulness. Clocks and calendars are tools, and like all tools they have their validity within that world where human Care seeks to regulate its projects. However, Care, in its essential temporal character, is not defined by clocks and calendars; on the contrary, clocks and calendars are useful tools because existence is *temporal* in its very nature.

Thus Heidegger would attempt to cut the ground from under the old philosophical quarrel as to whether time is "subjective" or "objective," by embracing neither alternative: both positions are wrong, but both seize aspects of the truth, it is only necessary to assign them their right place and order in the whole phenomenological structure of temporality. It was Aristotle who first enunciated this "vulgar" conception of time, which has dominated the minds of philosophers ever since, including Hegel and Bergson (who tried unsuccessfully, according to Heidegger, to escape its toils). But the history of philosophy also affords suspicion that it is not the complete truth about time, since other philosophers, from Plotinus and St. Augustine to Kant, have felt it necessary to make time "subjective." Though Heidegger claims to forswear—and incorporate—both alternatives, I think we shall find him belonging, in the end, to the latter camp—a contention which I shall come back to later.

Being essentially temporal, existence is also essentially *historical*. Parallel to temporality and time we have *historicity (Geschichtlichkeit)* and *history (Geschichte)*. Historicity is prior to history, as temporality is prior to time. Because man's existence is historical, he is able to write histories that represent history as a flow of events succeeding each other in time. Our existence is historical, whether we try to escape history or not, because, perpetually projecting a future, we transcend and yet return to our past. Perhaps Heidegger's chief contribution is to point out the significance of the future as defining our past. Tradition is not a *thing*, complete in itself, existing outside of the decision that places us in relation to it; on the contrary, we seize upon this or that aspect of the past—we create a tradition, in short—in view of the kind of future we are projecting. We choose ourselves in choosing our personal heroes out of history. T. S. Eliot, who has provided the best-known modern discussion of literary tradition, illustrates this point: the tradition that Eliot talked about as *the* tradition of English poetry was defined by the kind of poetry and criticism he himself was projecting for the future.* The contrast between the histories written by bourgeois and by socialist historians is the result of their different projects for the social future of mankind.

"Man makes history," said Marx, "but he does not make it out of whole cloth." Now the Marxist tradition has tended to affirm the second part of this proposition at the expense of forgetting altogether about the first. If Hei-

---

* Eliot himself has admitted this point in his essay, "The Music of Poetry," in *The Partisan Reader*, pp. 494–509.

degger takes only an abstractly theoretical account of the second part, his distinction is nevertheless to have fully elucidated the first part. The present, for Heidegger, is a making-present, and it is only as a derivative of this that we say man exists *in* the present. Historically his present is always the present of his *generation*. (This historical concept of the "generation" is borrowed from the writing of Dilthey.) Each generation feels its present as its historical *fate* (*Schicksal*). Far from being something external to which our existence passively submits, this fate is the very act of self-definition and self-projection by which we choose it as our fate. But Heidegger hardly notices the fact that one and the same generation may define for itself many and conflicting fates. *Our* generation, we say—and that may mean that *our* fate, the fate we choose, is to struggle against the whole of our generation. Heidegger's categories, of course, would apply to these historical conflicts within a given generation; the fact that he does not touch upon them shows something about himself rather than his system—namely, how greatly he lacks a sharp sense of history in its *social* and *political* dimensions. Whatever his merits, he remains first and last one of the Brahmans of the great German academic tradition—capable of the most childish self-deception (alongside of great learning and profound introspective imagination) in empirical matters; facts to remember in connection with his later brief allegiance to the Nazi party.

# III

## Existential Pathos and the Sense of Fact

No DOUBT, each age tends to think itself more problematic than its predecessors, for one's own existence must always seem more precarious than the past; but in our case we have witnessed such dissolution, accomplished or imminent, of so many structures of Western civilization that we seem to have good grounds for believing we are more doubt-ridden, more uncertain of ourselves, than man in the past. But despite our questioning, our multiplied sources of information, the twentieth century is still without any complete view of man, and in that direction Heidegger's is a document that cannot be neglected. Moreover, French existentialism is still a movement very much in progress, and it is impossible to foresee the precise directions it will take. We shall aim, therefore, at those criticisms that lead somewhere, permitting us to take over what is useful and reject the rest; that mark out the truly existential directions for the dark wood where speculation has lost the direct way.

Whatever our ensuing objections, they should not obscure the critical judgment that Heidegger's must be counted as one of the really important books of its time. Published in 1927, *Being and Time* belongs to the great productive period of postwar Germany, when the defeat of 1918 had actually quickened the spiritual life of the country —had given Germany its *décadence*, a state of spiritual refinement France went through after 1870, without, as after this last war, reducing social existence in Germany to the level of the animal. *Being and Time* exhibits Heidegger as a strange combination of remarkable genius and solemn actor (I almost said faker), and in his subsequent writings this latter quality seems to have become more predominant. One suspects that his intellectual fortunes may have followed the political graph of Germany over the last decade and a half, a period that witnessed the decline of the traditional and disciplined bourgeois existence from which the great German academic tradition had flowered. His seduction by the Nazis may be taken as one small incident in the accelerating bankruptcy of that class. Whether or not this intellectual and political parallel is too pat, only some future review of Heidegger's career will show; but we tend to doubt that any intellect, no matter how theoretical and rarefied its researches, could have escaped breathing the bad air of a corrupt national existence.

Which are the existential directions here? Where is the existential point of view confirmed, where abandoned? We address ourselves to these questions by turning immediately to Heidegger's initial ontological presentation itself—his claim that the analysis of human existence will provide a new key to the understanding of Being, in general. But this claim, I believe, is never realized, its persistence is a delusion, and the real value of the work lies rather in its concrete descriptions of human existence.

One proof of our contention would seem to be the fact that he has never published the second part of *Being and Time*, which was to have been the general theory of Being for which the first, the published part, was only the preliminary clearing of ground. The metaphysics that we do get in some of his subsequent works—in *On the Nature of Cause* (1929) and *What is Metaphysics?* (1933)—leaves it very questionable indeed that we have found here a new key to Being that will successfully upset the whole philosophic tradition of the West. In *What is Metaphysics?* he speaks of metaphysics as the fundamental *happening*, or experience, within human existence. If metaphysics has now become an experience, does not that imply that we are no longer to take it as furnishing us a doctrine—a structure of statements elucidating Being—and that Heidegger himself must have given up the claim to produce such a doctrine?

We are told, of course, that he wrote the second part of *Being and Time* before the first. The existence of this second part should not excite one's expectations too much; we can already guess its main directions from the indications toward the end of the first part. These indications deal with the subject of time, and as soon as one questions them, the crucial point in Heidegger's whole enterprise becomes exposed.

Now, Heidegger's whole treatment of the subject turns on the distinction between temporality and time, which we have already explained. By means of this distinction, and the phenomenological structure into which he integrates it,

Heidegger claims to cut the ground from under the old philosophic quarrel whether time is "objective" or "subjective." Is this really possible, without choosing one or the other, and does he do it? Certainly, we should be very much surprised if a German academic thinker escaped altogether the egotism of German philosophy, and even more surprised if Heidegger, who sees his philosophic mission in analogy with Kant's (see his *Kant and the Problem of Metaphysics*, 1934), should throw off completely the influence of that great idealist on this point. What is at issue here is not simply the question of time, however fascinating in itself, but the whole orientation of Heidegger's existentialism —and also the existentialism of Sartre, who follows Heidegger in this respect.

The fact is that Heidegger really relapses into idealism on this point. There is time, he says, because there is the temporality of human existence. This can only mean that if man did not exist, there would be no time. However different the terms by which he expresses it, and however much he seeks to bracket this question of objectivity versus subjectivity, his view of time, when we disengage its real content, is essentially subjective.

Thus he describes the traditional, realistic view of time, first expounded by Aristotle, as the "vulgar conception of time." What are the necessary logical ingredients of this "vulgar conception of time"? Principally: time exists so long as there is *change*, which need not all be the inner flow of consciousness. When Kant sought to locate time in the mind by abstracting it from the inner flow of consciousness, he was only drawing upon one example of change, and in respect to the relations of earlier and later the flow of thought is no different from any "objective" change in nature, like the earth's going around the sun. (Heidegger actually admits this point against Kant on p. 419 of *Being and Time*.) So long as there is change of any kind, conscious or not, there will be a time series based on the relation of earlier and later, and this will also contain present, past, future.*

But passing quickly beyond the abstract dialectic, let us plunge directly into the existential question itself. Is it possible really to grasp the full pathos of human existence if one accepts Heidegger's (and Sartre's) view of time? I think not, and I think that we get a far deeper view of the pathos of man's existence in time if we turn to another and older existentialist, Pascal, who says in one of his most famous fragments:

When I consider the short duration of my life, swallowed up in the eternity before and after, the little space which I fill, and even can see, engulfed in the infinite immensity of space of which I am ignorant, and which knows me not, I am frightened, and am astonished being here rather than there, why now rather than then.

Why now rather than then? This question haunts the existing individual as soon as he casts his vision over the immense extent and possibilities of human history. How, in fact, can Heidegger interpret the moment of my birth at all, since that is the *time* at which my *temporality* comes to be, and he makes the latter prior in nature? It is human pathos to

---

* This is not the occasion to go into the difficulties of constituting the time series. I hold with McTaggart against Russell that time must involve present, past, future; I am not aware of any valid argument that these require consciousness.

have been born "at this time" always, and man, coming into
the world, must always confront his time with something
of Hamlet's cry, "O cursed spite that ever I was born to set
it right!" It is also my pathos to be excluded from the centuries preceding me, from the heroes I love, whose actual
existence is a riddle at which I can only guess. I am cleft and
incomplete because I cannot know the future that will continue after me—will America, for example, ever have a
culture, can mankind achieve a decent and rational society?
—although this future, from which I am cut off, inhabits
my thinking at almost all moments. And even if men should
achieve some day a Utopia in comparison with what we
have now, they too will not escape this pathos, but will in
turn be cut off from their future; and if human development ceased, and there were no future toward which they
could turn, they would be even more pathetic. These
aspects of human pathos cannot be adequately expressed
within the context of Heidegger's distinction between temporality and time. Pascal strikes me as a superior existentialist here because he has a superior *sense of fact*. Analyzing
man's cares and anxieties, Pascal never leaves any doubt as
to the objective world of space and time in which he locates
man's being. Man is located against the background of "the
silence of those infinite spaces," against the teeming world
of microscopic animalcules, Cleopatra's nose, and the grain
of sand in Cromwell's kidney.*

---

* Heidegger distinguishes between spatiality and space in a manner
analogous to his distinction between temporality and time. I think the
quotation from Pascal can be used to develop the same dialectic
against this distinction too.

Pascal, it seems, grasped certain of Heidegger's concepts better than Heidegger himself. In his concepts of *Geworfenheit* and *Faktizität*, Heidegger attempted to express two essential aspects of human contingency: that man is thrown (*geworfen*) into a world he never made and his existence undertaken amid conditions that are there, given, factual (*faktisch*, hence *Faktizität*). Accordingly, we propose to turn Heidegger on his head, and say: *Man is temporal because he happens to have been thrown into a world in which there is time.* Human consciousness does not add time to the universe, but only the consciousness of time. To be sure, consciousness makes man's temporality unique among all beings, but only because through consciousness he grasps his own existence as immediately spread out in time. What, after all, is the whole point of Kierkegaard's polemic against Hegel, if not that existentialism loses its pungency, its sense of fact, when it relapses into idealism?

## Phenomenology, and the Phenomenological Surface

The fact that Heidegger relapses above into the egotism of German philosophy brings up one of the principal tensions within his system—which we mentioned earlier but postponed discussing. One extraordinary feature of his approach is its sweeping "objectivity": he does not begin to philosophize from a pure Ego—an inner consciousness abstracted from all its spiritual conditions—but with a world and other people that are immediately *there*. But it seems that Heidegger has not really grasped the extent to which he is radically overturning phenomenology, and phenomenological method, as understood and practiced by Husserl.

Let us look at Husserl first. He begins from the natural standpoint of everyday life, which is a continuous perceiving of an external world, or environment, surrounding us:

For me real objects are there, definite, more or less familiar . . . I can let my attention wander from the writing-table I have just seen and observed, through the unseen portions of the room behind my back to the veranda, into the garden, to the children in the summer-house, and so forth, to all the objects concerning which I precisely know that they are there and yonder in my immediate coperceived surroundings—a knowledge which has nothing of conceptual thinking in it, and first changes into clear intuiting with the bestowing of attention, and even then only partially and for the most part very imperfectly.

Into this natural perceiving state of everyday life Husserl wishes to introduce a radically different standpoint: namely, the Cartesian doubt about the external world—though, to be sure, his use of this doubt will be different from Descartes's. I say to myself: it is possible I am being deceived, there is no table here, I only have the illusion of perceiving it; I appear to hear shouts from the garden, but there are really no children there. And so on, for all the objects in my "real" world of ordinary experience. What remains? Only the experiences of consciousness itself. The real external world of natural normal experience has been *disconnected*, or *bracketed*, from consciousness. Husserl does not raise this "doubt" in order to cast uncertainty upon our belief in the existence of a real world outside our consciousness; it is only his means of bracketing off, in turn, the whole manifold realm of consciousness, which is now to become the domain investigated by the rigorous philosophic discipline he calls phenomenology.

Let us examine this bracketing with historical eyes for a moment. Ancient skepticism—I am talking about the pre-Aristotelian skeptics—did not travel this road of doubt, though it went farther along other paths. How is this? How is it they did not doubt the external world and other people, although one fine Sophist went so far as to doubt the possibility of communication itself and ended up by wiggling his finger in order to express himself? At the very moment they felt their language incapable of coping with the eternal flux of nature, these Heraclitean Greeks, healthy and natural children, could not bring themselves to doubt the existence itself of nature. They philosophized in the market place, in the open air and the good Mediterranean sunlight, and it would have struck them as insanity, rather than doubt, not to recognize where one was and the people around one. Modern philosophy, since Descartes, has smelled of the private study and the library, where a man, in his solitude, perpetually pinching himself to see whether he is dreaming, can entertain, or pretend to entertain, beliefs he could not hold in the open air and light of a city square.

What will do us for a market place? Washington Square on a fine spring afternoon, where we are lucky to find an empty seat to squeeze into, and this neighbor, whose existence we are to bracket, probably is sticking his elbow in our ribs. Here, now, what does this bracketing mean? By a process of intense self-hypnosis I may be able to work myself into a state where I suspend my beliefs, my perceptions seem illusions, and I can even feel, like a Hindu sage, that all this is a dream—and a dream from which I shall never awaken. But this state would only be one among many, and we have to ask: What does this bracketing mean—logi-

cally? Simply this: that the proposition, "There are no people here in the park," is not logically self-contradictory. But
the question remains, whether I do not *in fact know* that
this proposition, however self-consistent, is actually false.
Husserl tells us we are to put within brackets absolutely
everything that is given; but where does the given end, and
suppose the reality of the world, as well as its appearance,
is given? I am to place within brackets not only the objects
of my present perceptions, but of my memories of this
place, of other people, of my total experience. The brackets
bulge and break, the mass of the world is too great to be
contained by them. Under *these* complete and concrete
conditions (which cannot be expressed in their totality), I
do certainly know that I am in this square, and that there
are other people here. And if this certain knowledge is
given, then its object, the reality of the world and other
people, is also given.*

Our argument seems to me a quite rigorous one, a reduction to the absurd: if we attempt to bracket the world completely, the brackets break down, and we are necessarily
led from a bracketed consciousness to a world outside consciousness. The mind is inextricably tangled with things,
mind and world are given together. A classical position in
fact, already expressed in Aristotle's great statement, "the
mind is in a manner all things." We have but to plunge into

---

* This argument rests upon G. E. Moore's analytic of common
sense, and its dialectic defense, in detail, may be safely left to Moore
or his followers. Moore's, by the way, is one more of the modern
efforts to consummate the death of Descartes. Moore has arrived at
the position that he knows certain things concerning which he cannot
give any adequate explanation *how* it is he knows them. The next step
of the Cambridge School would be to declare that its philosophy is
inadequate to what it knows. That would require more daring.

consciousness and we find ourselves among things and within the world.

The procedure of bracketing served Husserl as a propaedeutic: a means of isolating the fact of consciousness as a domain for philosophic investigation. We do not question its usefulness for that—and particularly for guarding against some materialistic misunderstandings of consciousness. What we question is the phenomenological orientation itself as a complete and final attitude of mind, particularly its usefulness as soon as we want real knowledge—knowledge that bites into reality and does not remain merely on the surface. In the hands of Sartre, French existentialism has tended to become all too phenomenological. The dwelling on the phenomenological surface can become a kind of virginity of mind. Where does the complete phenomenological attitude lead us? In aesthetics, for example? To theories of the aesthetic surface, formalism, beauty as disinterested contemplation, etc., etc.—theories which leave the complete work of art inexplicable, and were already refuted by Stendhal and Nietzsche. In psychology? To Sartre's attempt to explain the anti-Semite by a dialectical manipulation of two very abstract categories of Being, which hardly touches the facts of anti-Semitism, and where psychoanalysis gives us real knowledge because it dares to go below the surface. And what of those "eidetic," or formal, disciplines of mathematics, which were really the goal of Husserl's aspirations? What a deal of pushing and pulling on the wharves of the Italian cities of the Renaissance, what hauling and carting of the new commerce, raising and lowering by cranes, winches, and pulleys, before Galileo could think of forces with any degree of abstractness, and modern mathematics come into the world—hand in hand, notice, with modern physics, from which it passed into formal purity only much later. Existentialism (of the Sartrian school) has not profited enough from Nietzsche, who understood that knowledge is a form of aggression against nature, a breaking into Being, a diving beneath the surface. Can the whole of modern science be understood historically except as the child of the Renaissance, when man, giving up the passive religious contemplation of the Middle Ages, enters upon the historical scene as the conqueror of nature, as a doer of deeds? And we may recall, finally, the words of Hegel against Kant, in a slightly different connection, but which apply against Kant's twentieth-century follower, Husserl: "Clearly, behind the so-called curtain, which is to hide the inner world (below the surface of appearances) there is nothing to be seen if we ourselves do not go behind there."

If Heidegger has not pursued our argument about bracketing, we might say it is really implicit in his abrupt plunge *in medias res,* beginning with Being-in-the-world and other people. But we should also say that he had not grasped the radical significance of his starting point. For what follows if consciousness and world (not Heidegger's *Welt,* which is only a part of a phenomenological structure, but the real world external to consciousness) are given together? Then man—conscious existence, *Dasein*—is only a being among other beings, and it is an illusion to seek for a key to Being in general from the analyses of human Care, temporality, etc. Heidegger cannot hope to philosophize in any fashion parallel to the Copernican Revolution of Kant (who attempted to constitute the world from the nature of the knowing subject), for his initial point of departure has already taken him beyond any possible Kantian approach. (This is the fundamental tension we spoke about earlier.) But it seems impossible that a German should overcome altogether his youthful discipline in Kant.

This illusion concerning the key to Being is shown, once and for all, by the final conclusion toward which the 400 pages of Heidegger's analysis points: since human existence is essentially temporal, woven warp and woof of future, past and present, he goes on to say that time is the meaning of Being in general. But what does this mean? Simply, that it would be impossible to conceive a nontemporal Being. But suppose there were an essentially unchanging (and therefore nontemporal) thing anywhere in or out of the universe. Here the actual existence is not in question, but only the possibility. (Sartre flatly denies this possibility, but without proof, and Heidegger, if he is serious, would have to make the same denial.) But I see nothing self-contradictory in the conception of a nontemporal Being, and so I must find here, as it would be anyway, the inference from human being to Being, in general, invalid.

Another illustration of the same point could be taken from his analysis of causality and the principle of sufficient reason in his essay, *On the Nature of Cause*. Heidegger begins with a brief historical review of the problem in Leibnitz and Schopenhauer, and then goes on to say that the problem must be posed within the context of human existence itself. Man's nature is to transcend his past, and in this act of transcending he wills to ground his own existence —such is Heidegger's account of the basis of the Principle of Sufficient Reason. Now it is all very well to point out with Nietzsche (it is from him that Heidegger is borrowing here) that causes, laws, reasons follow from man's will to seek a ground; but this is absolutely no answer at all to the question that Leibnitz, and other philosophers, were raising. They wished to know whether such a thing as causality did in fact hold of nature, and (in Leibnitz's case, particularly) whether there was a cause for nature in its totality. Heidegger says absolutely nothing to answer those questions; instead he turns to an analysis of the self-transcending existence of man, and it should be quite clear that once the problem is posed within that context, no answer at all can be given to the older problems.

We come back to the same criticism (and perhaps it is only one criticism we have throughout) in connection with the essay *What is Metaphysics?* Metaphysics, he says, is the fundamental experience of human existence, arrived at through anxiety, which lays bare the basic question: *Why is there anything at all rather than nothing?* There the essay ends, but if this is a question, presumably there is some answer, whether we are *de facto* able to know it or not, or else the question is meaningless. Heidegger does not deal with this question in its own terms, but as part of the phenomenology of human existence: Man's being is perpetually suspended over this question, which he can neither remove nor answer. But the very nature of the question is that it points beyond the human condition and whatever phenomenological brackets we place about that condition. It is the situation of the religious decision with Kierkegaard, of Pascal's wager; and Pascal is right, we must wager: even if we choose to hover permanently within it, we have answered this question, and moved beyond the brackets. If Heidegger holds there is nothing higher than human existence, he has already answered that there is no reason why anything at all exists rather than nothing, and this answer takes us beyond phenomenology, for it is a decision on the universe itself and its reality. The dialectical irony is that Heidegger's systematic thought ends by arriving at a question, which, so long as he remains within that system, he can neither answer nor reject.

## The One

Once we have traversed our preceding arguments, and placed man among things and within a world (in a far more real, or realist, sense than Heidegger), then any empirical source of knowledge becomes relevant, and we must question Heidegger's analysis of this One—the anonymous individual of the crowd—from the viewpoint of the psychoanalyst.

Heidegger tells us that this banal character of everyday existence is fundamentally guiltless: the One avoids, as much as he can, the really human responsibility of guilt. He regards his guilt *as a thing*—something like a toothache, which he is concerned only to get rid of. The One does not have the "will to be guilty"—the essential note of conscience that defines authentic existence. Now, the psychoanalyst would tell us, on the contrary, that this banal individual is ridden with guilt; that he is choking with the repressions, resentments, and guilt that arises from these; and, finally, that he can reach a really human level by willing to throw off a good deal of his guilt, particularly the parts that arise from the invalid prescriptions of social fear, the *mores* of the human hive. Hence the voice of conscience would become the will *not* to be guilty—the will to conquer one's guilt and rise above it. Here Nietzsche speaks against Heidegger.

The One, we have seen, escapes from his fallen state, and rises to authentic existence through the experience of his complete isolation as a Self confronting death. Afterward the public world is restored to him, but with a difference. (Heidegger's version, we have observed, of the Kierke-gaardian Repetition.) Heidegger, however, hardly deals with this point adequately. If a realization of our complete solitude in the face of death is necessary for securing an authentic existence, it is also true that we must realize our authenticity in communication and exchange with others. Now, this criticism has often been made, but never in such a fashion as to get at the source of Heidegger's inadequacy. His trouble is that, though he begins by positing our existence as an existence-with-others, what he describes is an abstraction and not the concrete coexistence of daily life. Everyday life is not that *undifferentiated public* existence that he describes as the existence of the One; our banality is not the anonymity of the crowd, except for certain moments; we move within smaller communities rather than an abstract public world at large; within groups, circles of friends and enemies, full of the passion of personal intrigue, differences, back-biting, gossip, and now and then the possible occasions of love, the joys and communication in friendship. Hence it is within that concrete and extremely personal context (from which we start) that we must hammer out our own truthfulness and authenticity. Otherwise the absolute solitude with which we resolutely confront death becomes a neurotic escape from the task of being a person, ourself, among the other persons we know.

There is another tension (but perhaps it returns, at bottom, to the one we have been talking about) in Heidegger's system, which we may baptize as the opposition between Dilthey and Husserl. Husserl had claimed for phenomenology an absolute rigor and universality: absolutely self-contained, embracing its own principles, it reaches truths that are not relative to the given historical epoch and culture. Now the question is whether these claims can be maintained in the case of the phenomenological analysis of such a subject as death, for example. Heidegger, insofar as he is practicing phenomenology, is claiming to produce an analysis of death, and the mode in which man confronts it, which is valid for all times and cultures. Dilthey, on the other hand, had arrived at what we might call an ontology of historical relativism: no system can embrace existence totally and finally, and hence every philosophical system is only a "philosophical fragment." Hence philosophy must always take its origin from the pre-philosophical from which it can never cut itself completely off, and this pre-philosophical stage of existence changes with human history. From this point of view, I doubt whether Heidegger's analysis of death can pretend to any absolute phenomenological universality. In ages of faith, where belief in an after life is assumed as a matter of fact, the way in which man confronts death is altogether different from what Heidegger describes. The medieval Christian, believing exultantly or fearfully in the next life, could face death as the simple gateway to another world, and he did not fear the losing of this existence so much as the loss of happiness hereafter. Clearly, Heidegger is analyzing the consciousness of death in our historical epoch—which has, precisely, foregone the hope of immortality.

Thus we have found Heidegger's to be a system full of the tensions of opposed orientations. In a sense what he attempts to do is to bring Pascal and Kierkegaard together with the whole Western tradition of ontology from Aristotle through the Schoolmen. But in this matter we should remember Pascal's careful avoidance of metaphysics. Pascal is more aware of the unique character of his existential task: he never takes his eye off the fact that he is addressing the individual person, who exists in uneasiness and anxiety and longs for *his own* salvation, and that this uneasy individual is not looking for a general metaphysical system. Here, again, we may invoke our old friend, the Underground Man. What concern is it of his to have a key to all Being— especially when we find that the key really unlocks nothing? He wants something for himself, for his own unique existence, and it is this need to which both Pascal and Kierkegaard address themselves—whether or not what they offer will satisfy our Underground Man of today. In short, the essential point of view in Pascal and Kierkegaard is purer.

The presence of all these tensions within Heidegger's system is a witness of the extraordinary breadth of his philosophic culture, of the number of influences he has tried to absorb, but I also take it as the sign that the great tradition of German philosophy has here reached its stage of late August, overripe, ready for decline. And perhaps— now with Germany's destruction as a culture—Heidegger is the last philosopher of that tradition: if there is to be any future German philosophy, it will have to overcome a good deal of its tradition. A sign that we have here reached a late stage of cultural development is Heidegger's peculiar fascination by the pre-Socratics, for what else is this but that longing for the primitive that always characterizes the stage of overripeness? Heidegger seeks to resuscitate the thought of the pre-Socratics because he finds in them a consciousness, not yet broken up by analysis, of the unity in existence of man and his world. But we can find this unity, and more consciously articulate, at least as late as Aristotle, and the wish to capture the spirit of his predecessors is perhaps only a gratuitous and unnecessary aspiration toward primitivism. Heidegger's longing for the primitive strikes us as an extraordinary accompaniment of certain primitive tendencies that run through modern art and modern literature. Perhaps Western culture as a whole has become overripe.

# IV

## The Historical Frame: Existentialism as a "Philosophic Fragment"

THE ANCIENT SAGE THALES, while walking and contemplating the stars, fell into a well. A serving girl, who stood nearby, greeted this with jeers and laughter. She was no intellectual, obviously, otherwise she might have paused to think that what she had just observed was the history of philosophy as comedy. Thales was no dreamer, far from it; we are told he went on to establish the first monopoly recorded in history, cornering the olive market in Greece; I like to think he did this because he had been so annoyed by the girl's laughter. Now, this well is actuality itself, and the comedy is that the philosopher is always falling down it. Philosophers have always been haunted by the goal of a complete system that would grasp its own principles in a systematic and self-justifying rigor; but they never quite get free from dependence upon the pre-philosophic stages of language and thought, from which they would take off into the upper atmosphere. They too are children of their epoch, and the system turns out in the end a "philosophic fragment" (in Kierkegaard's sense). Probably it never occurred to Spinoza, as he walked past the stock exchange in Amsterdam, that his thought was particularly related to these counting houses; his attention was on his own stars, the system he was developing *more geometrico* from necessary first principles; but we who compare his treatment of the human passions with the medieval treatment by St. Thomas Aquinas easily see a relation to those stock exchanges and the nascent capitalism of the Renaissance. Suppose that history had not accumulated for us since Thales' day, what kind of philosophic questions would we be asking? If we did not know any more science than he, we would probably still be asking with him whether water is the substance of all things.

By turning to history as our summing up, we do not pass to something extraneous to our argument, but simply continue our previous criticism, in the direction of the concrete and actual, bringing abstractions face to face with the sense of fact, exhibiting philosophy itself in its existential incompleteness, as it opens out upon the world in which it came into birth. This is but to bring the existential point of view to its completeness, and that is why we place this bit of history at the end rather than the beginning. No doubt, this may involve some cynicism toward philosophy, but it is a kind of cynicism already expressed in Kierkegaard and Nietzsche; and here, as with women, perhaps it is only cynicism that permits us to love philosophy wisely.

Nevertheless a very long chain of causes stretches from those Amsterdam counting houses to Spinoza's treatment of the passions; we do not deny it, but neither do we intend to become involved in one of the most intricate and difficult quarrels of historical theory. Instead, we simply assume that human consciousness exists completely in its historical epoch, and ask what correlations that permits us to make. Perhaps a cultural event is "explained" only in the sense and to the degree that the correlations with other historical events are suitably dense and coherent.

The historical period we have been dealing with here is obviously the period of Romanticism in Europe, and we should like to take as integral a view of it as we can of the Renaissance—an impossibility perhaps, since we are still in the midst of this period, and its final horizon, still in the future, is darkened to us. What we can distinguish as a Renaissance consciousness is already found in the painting of the fourteenth century, but it does not appear in the philosophers until the fifteenth, sixteenth, and seventeenth centuries. The artists are the sensitive reeds that first vibrate to the new currents which flow into the historical epoch and give it precisely the feeling and exultation that it is new. The Renaissance artists themselves need not have been expressly aware of this new attitude toward existence, which they possessed only as an ingredient in their way of seeing the world; it became conscious and explicit in the philosophers. If Romantic art was also new and revolutionary, then it too must have grasped some radically new areas of human existence, which the philosophers have subsequently been struggling to bring to explicit conceptual expression.

## Art

Modern art—that art that begins with the Romantic movement—has become characterized by its progressive morbidity, its sensational and startling character, the presentation of human life in its extreme situations. The art produced in the first part of the eighteenth century, fundamentally classical in its directions, deals with the human in its universal dimensions, with wit, manners, morals: man as a creature of a definite nature, at the center of a world which is ordered and understood, and does not exist on the edge of chaos. The novel, which is so peculiarly a modern literary form, exists, but it has not yet become the modern novel. Thus Fielding's *Tom Jones* and Stendhal's *The Red and the Black* are both versions of the picaresque novel dealing with a young man's adventures in the world, but it would be hard to find two works more different in fundamental outlook. Where Fielding's subject is the existence of human foibles against the background of a definite conception of human nature, Stendhal has introduced a new and daring *sense of experiment* with man: all the stable forms of society are seen to be perched over the chaos of the irrational, the arbitrary, and the contingent in man himself.

We also hear these tones of discord in the new music. Turning from the melancholy portions of Handel's "Water Music" to one of Beethoven's last quartets, we have entered a different world. In Handel, the emotion is completely contained and formed; sad and melancholy, it is torn neither by doubts nor uncertainties; we seem to be present at some recognized social occasion and chamber of mourning,

where our grief is shared, in essential human communion, by
other people there. When we hear one of Beethoven's last
quartets, we seem to be alone. The solid human world
whose contours were present in Handel has dissolved into
questions, doubts, anxieties. Through this dissolution of accepted status, the naked ego has come into the world, the
individual has been born into bourgeois society with all its
pressures and conflicts. This is the music of anxiety, and,
as such, it strikes us as peculiarly *modern* music.

A French critic has found in the paintings of Picasso a
"terrible and modern beauty." An important chapter of
intellectual history could be written on this particular use
of "modern"—the peculiar reverberations and associations
it has for contemporary ears. When Baudelaire wrote of
Flaubert, and found *Madame Bovary* "so profoundly *modern*" (his italics), he was illustrating this meaning that seems
to set the art of the last 150 years off from the great bulk of
earlier art. It is hard to know just when this peculiar awareness of modernity begins, but the first conscious uses of it I
find in Stendhal, when he poses such questions for his age
as, "What kind of art do we, we moderns of the year 1830,
want?"

Now, this sense of the modern is quite different from
what launched the seventeenth-century debate in France
and England about the relative merits of ancients and
moderns. That debate arose in the historical period when the
new national literatures had already developed to the point
where they had produced works that invited comparison
with the great classics of the ancient world. However, the
comparison was between works on the same terrain of consciousness—works of the same genus, which were essen-

tially comparable one with another: Milton with Virgil, for example. But in Baudelaire's use of "modern" there is the feeling of something new in kind, strictly incomparable with what has gone before.

In this sense, it might not be wrong to describe modern art, where it has succeeded, as more *profound* than the art of the past, provided we do not take this to mean "superior" or "more perfect," since profundity may be purchased by the loss of other qualities. Dostoevsky is often more profound than Shakespeare, but we should not say that he was a greater writer. What does this modern profundity mean? In what sense does Beethoven seem to us more profound than Handel? Because what we hear in Beethoven seems at times just on the edge of articulate sound, as if the music were hovering over the inexpressible and drawing it into itself. The experience with which modern art struggles has become more frantic, homeless, solitary, speechless. The pages in literature of which I am reminded by some of the last quartets are certain passages in Kafka's *Journals*—and precisely those passages where he talks of the mystery of suffering and expression, of suffering become lucid in expression, the speechless and the articulate. What we hear, then, in Beethoven are the opening chords in the *Age of Neurosis*.

## Society

But what art gives expression to has come into being through other causes. Two large-scale historical events run parallel to the movement we are considering: (1) the Industrial Revolution, and the consequent establishment of the bourgeoisie (which, of course, as a class had emerged long before) at the helm of modern society; and (2) the uneasiness and tensions within bourgeois society, its inability to solve its problems, its rapid and startling decline within this century, and the consequent despair in the midst of this class.

The bourgeois brings with him into history a scrupulous concern for the individual. But this only opens the subject to us, since it is necessary to go on to explain why this concern for the individual was content to exercise itself in the eighteenth century in the field of social and political criticism, whereas in the nineteenth century it is turned in upon personal existence in and of itself, and philosophers begin to go in search of the concrete and existential.

The French Revolution brought into existence what Karl Jaspers has aptly termed "the epochal consciousness." Kant himself remarked apropos of the events of 1789:

Such a phenomenon in history can never be forgotten, inasmuch as it has disclosed in human nature the rudiments of and capacity for better things which, prior to this, no student of political science had deduced from the previous course of human events.

This epochal consciousness begets the modern historical sense. History, as a critical and scientific study, really began in the eighteenth century, but that century, still too much under the influence of Plutarch, tended still to think of history as "philosophy teaching by examples," to cite Bolingbroke's words. The modern historical sense came into being after the French Revolution had shown that human society might be remade from top to bottom by the actions of men. Henceforth the most deeply embedded social forms could appear as potentially transitory, and human existence in the past could be seen as relative always to its historical conditions of social and economic organization. But if society now appeared capable of such profound transformations for human betterment, it could also, on the other hand, be seen as hovering on the edge of the precipice, capable of some really radical smash-up and consequent regression to a lower phase. Hence this epochal consciousness brings to birth in the nineteenth century a peculiarly new kind of prophet of despair or degeneration—Stendhal, De Tocqueville, Nietzsche, Burkhardt—that we have seen multiply in the historical pessimists of the twentieth century.

The existential notion of "authenticity" itself has a great deal to tell us about the progress of life under the bourgeois order. Let us speak for a moment like Nietzsche, who used to ask of other thinkers, "What is *his* truth, and how does it measure against *my* truth?"—the point being that we completely grasp another doctrine only by taking the measure of the man who has brought it to utterance. What, then, is *their* truth—the truth of Heidegger and Jaspers—when they enunciate their category of an authentic life? We catch the clearest glimpse of what is historically involved from Jaspers' own book about our age, *Man in the Modern World*. The category of authenticity is the fear which the bourgeois, the academic Brahman, expresses at the encroachment of the masses, of the technological agglomeration of the life-order under modern society, upon his own spiritual existence. This is also what we find expressed in the writings of the Spanish philosopher Ortega y Gasset. Authenticity could not become such a compelling concept if modern society did not make it more and more difficult, almost impossible, to live a human life.

This is *their* truth, but let us not fall into the error that by placing a man's truth we rob it of its veracity. Marx prophesied rightly the breakdown of capitalist society and the consequent decay of the bourgeois class itself, but we must recognize that the aristocrats and the bourgeois Brahmans have been on their own side quite as good prophets about the quality of life that is now succeeding Europe's bourgeois civilization. I am writing the history of the next hundred years, said Nietzsche, and that history will be one of nihilism; this was as good a prophecy as Marx's though Nietzsche, of course, failed to predict that when this nihilism came it would express itself in his own language of power, both in Germany and Russia! No, we cannot rob *their* truth of its truthfulness: authenticity has become a profoundly meaningful, indeed inescapable, category for all of us because the modern world and the modern city with their congestion, standardization, regimentation in and out of war, beat upon us all, threatening to reduce our personalities to mere figments and shadows. The man of the early eighteenth century (the man of leisure and means, that is, for the masses were not thought of as falling within the really human pale) could not have felt that the achievement of a personality was his task in life. He took the fact of his own personality for granted.

Now, there are many historical sources for this uneasiness toward the possibility of achieving a human life. The crudest and most powerful cause may be the fact that man has not yet shown himself capable of controlling and shaping in some rational way the technological order, or disorder, that surrounds and strangles modern life like a rampant jungle of metallic liana plants.

The Industrial Revolution, on its intellectual rather than directly social side, is the triumphant emergence of technology at the forefront of modern life. Technology is the visible and material incarnation of science in the social life. Modern science had, of course, begun to exist long before this period. But by this time the scientific *Weltanschauung* comes to the fore: science has become the chief intellectual activity of modern man. The newcomer threatens the previous incumbent: religion. The Enlightenment had already been at work in the eighteenth century, and accomplished its task of religious criticism in the name of Reason. Henceforth, the nineteenth century will be engaged in the passionate struggle to recapture, or to demolish finally, what is actually in the process of withering away.

Hence, the startling fact that in this broad movement we are considering, science becomes a "problem" to philosophy in a way never seen before. No doubt, there are certain antirationalist strains present throughout this movement. But perhaps too much attention may have been called to them, since the presence of antirationalism does not characterize this movement essentially. When a philosopher like Bergson—criticized perhaps as much as any figure here for antirationalism—speaks of certain deficiencies of the "intelligence" in comparison with "intuition," we must also remember that the body of his writings, both in form and concentration, witness an intense devotion to the intellect. Nevertheless, in this movement science does appear as something to be "transcended" in one way or another, or to be

reintegrated within the total of human experience. Kierkegaard is the most dramatic: in his category of the "exception" he announces that individual existence, with its dread,
freedom, and absolute decisions, forever escapes all science.
Nietzsche thinks that the results of science call for a desperate affirmation on the part of man, the hero, who would
look truth in the face. Whitehead would replace science
within the fundamental "feeling" pattern of human experience; Heidegger would see science itself as a passion and
mode of human existence; Dewey attempts, in a more mat-
ter-of-fact way, to reintegrate science into the biological
and cultural matrix.

To put it another way, Dewey seeks to give science its
concrete and proper place in the human community.
Science has become a "problem" not simply because its appearance has upset the intellectual economy by undermin-
ing traditional religious beliefs. This disruption in the intellectual economy is itself a reflection of the disruption in
the actual social economy that science, in its visible incarnation as technology, has brought. Science remains something
to be reintegrated into the intellectual economy, as its material counterpart has not been integrated into the social
economy. Technology has raised immeasurably the productive forces of modern society, but at the same time produces
the most drastic convulsions and contradictions in the form
of crises, pauperization of the masses, uprooting of the peas-
antry, and wars which, in their mechanical horror, virtually
make war itself a new historical phenomenon. It is questionable whether science would have become such a passionate
"problem" for philosophy if its social embodiment in the
form of technology had not become such an insoluble prob-

lem to modern society. In his vision of this social aspect, Dewey outstrips all the other philosophers we have touched upon here.

Examination of Romantic literature deepens this correlation. Romanticism appears first as a literary phenomenon in England, precisely the country in which the industrial revolution makes its first appearance. Romanticism emerges as an intense longing for return to the past, and the particular past longed for is the medieval past. This is a remarkable phenomenon. The first Romantic literature appears in England after 1750, and it is precisely at this time that the development of factories and industrialism is in process of uprooting the peasant from his feudal and medieval past. This past slumbered around the Englishman in his villages, in the thousand inherited habits and customs of their daily life— slumbered unnoticed, its medieval origin being on the whole hidden; but at the moment when this richness of rural life is about to be submerged under industrialism, the medieval past—"Merrie England"—acquires an astounding enchantment. The irony of history could not be more pronounced.

But not only when it seeks return to the medieval past, with all its imagined folk-richness, is Romanticism in quest of a renewed intensity for ordinary existence. Medievalism is only a station on the way in pursuit of the intensity of life in general. Distant times and places acquire an intoxicating glamor precisely because industrialism has impoverished the richness of ordinary existence. A philosophy which gives itself completely to concrete existence takes its point of departure from the same fundamental impulse: the philosopher too is seeking to resuscitate the richness of existence, to restore its passion, decision, and meaning. Kierkegaard announces this goal with the greatest possible clearness and decision.

Romanticism did not stop at literature, it entered life in a very direct way. The Romantic revolt could not have confined itself merely to the heroes of its fiction; its existence overflowed the realms of imagination and art, and posed the problem of life directly. Rimbaud, who occurs in the ripe or overripe stage of the movement, becomes a kind of parable of all the extreme situations posed by the whole of Romanticism. His history is a passionate incarnation of the categories that existential philosophers have been struggling with on their own field—the Absolute Decision, Resoluteness, Choice of Oneself. Romanticism posed the problem of the individual as it had never been posed before in human history. Considered from this point of view, Heidegger's philosophy represents the scholasticism, the final anatomy, of the Romantic individual.

## Religion

It has been obvious through all the foregoing that the dissolution of a world of status has also been the dissolution of a received religious framework. Perhaps the decay of religion over the last two centuries has been the most profound event touching the life of man—at least, his spiritual and conscious life—though, as we have seen, there have been more drastic changes modifying the rest of his being. With this traditional religious framework speculative philosophy went hand in hand; and the passing away of speculative philosophy—the growing unwillingness even to attempt it—entails more consequences than I believe most rationalist philosophers have been able or willing to see.

But we must see this disappearance of the accepted religious frame on the level of existence first, for the withering away of religion does not operate only on the intellectual level of belief. Religion surrounded the daily life of man, sanctifying his birth and death, making the ordinary occasions of life resonant with the tremendous echoes of supernatural existence. One cannot forget, for example, the extent to which Christianity exists as a fundamental mode of feeling and thinking in such "rationalist" writers of the eighteenth century as Pope and Swift. We see now that Swift (and this is true of Pope too) was sometimes penetrated by the rationalism of his epoch much more than he was aware of: from his enthusiastic picture of the completely rational Houyhnhnms we hardly get the impression that they have any need of a Savior to redeem them by his death, whereas a Savior could have no meaning for the Yahoos since they are beyond redemption. But Christianity was never *consciously* in question for Swift, it was his accepted view of life and the world, taken over along with the rationalist prejudices of his epoch, and he felt no tension at all between the two inheritances. So Pope on his deathbed received extreme unction quite as a matter of course—although a friend remarked that it was simply Socrates' sacrifice of a cock to Aesculapius.

Some historians and critics have written of the conflict between Romanticism and Classicism as if this latter were simply a repetition of ancient Greece and Rome. The fact is that a fundamental Christian content lies at the basis of

Classicism both in England and France, and the literary models from classical antiquity are superposed upon this content. Romanticism is not simply the rejection of the "unities," the heroic couplet, the Alexandrine, or any other accepted literary convention or form; its opposition to Classicism takes place at a deeper level: The Romantic sensibility, the Romantic passion for existence, posit an attitude toward life which rejects this inherited Christian content; and although one early wave of Romanticism came in the form of a religious revival, it pursued mainly the intoxicating trappings of religion, liturgy, incense, stained glass, and medieval cathedrals. It is no accident that the acutest of modern critics, T. S. Eliot, joins his affirmation of classicism in literature to an affirmation of Christianity in religion; Eliot sees very well that his acceptance of a Christian view of life involves the rejection of romanticism. Eighteenth-century man did not feel this passionate necessity to explore concrete human existence in itself as a subject matter for philosophy; the Romantic quest for the intensity of experience was, in part, its compensation for the loss of the eternal horizons of religion—as the Christian sinner plunges desperately into the intensity of his sin believing the price he pays for it is an eternal loss. Kierkegaard is the only believing Christian among the figures we have considered, and his exception confirms our rule. For what is involved in Kierkegaard's lifelong struggle against institutional Christendom but the fact that the Christian attitude toward life can no longer be presupposed as a datum, that it has been completely forgotten by everybody, and must be struggled for to be recovered?

The fact that these historical phenomena with which one

is bound to correlate this philosophical movement are still the main forces conditioning, whether for good or evil, our own lives, is a witness of how decisive the problems still are for our own thinking and living. If most of these correlations have been already familiar, this does not mean that they have already yielded their last drop of insight for our own particular uses. On the contrary, we are still in an uncertain relation to Romanticism: no one has yet delivered at our feet in a neat bundle the final results, conclusions, and generalizations, which would permit us to declare a chapter finally closed. Every fundamental problem of our contemporary existence sends us back to this historical context; and, questioning this historical context for its meaning, we are brought back in turn to the problem of our own existence.

*We come back to our Underground Man. He has been with us throughout, and it is obvious from the preceding history that we have not yet gotten rid of him. One of his most powerful talents is to be capable of the most startling reincarnations, and in various guises and disguises he has been haunting the literature of this century. He is the pro- tagonist of Céline's* Journey to the End of Night, *of Sartre's* La Nausée, *and with a slightly different temperament, he is Meursault, the hero of Albert Camus's* The Stranger. *And if those incoherent creatures of thunder and lightning, Wil- liam Faulkner's heroes, were to think, they too would ex- hibit an underground consciousness.*

*He also walks the streets of real life. I used often to meet him in New York cafeterias during the long Depression of the thirties, and even now I still hear him speaking through the voice of some of our disabused intellectuals condemned to the penal servitude of American life.*

*But this Underground Man is dangerous—let us not for- get that. His reappearances are not always philosophical and harmless. It is painful, but one has to report the truth that in the twentieth century he also became a Nazi func- tionary and burned bodies at Buchenwald; and he has operated as a Stalinist official herding thousands of Euro- peans to their death.*

*Since he originally came on the scene, another newcomer has appeared, ready with new proposals in his behalf. "I can cure him," says the psychoanalyst. The newcomer has performed some redoubtable feats, for which he has very serious claims on our attention; but we are inclined to be a little skeptical that he can turn this particular trick anywhere in the very near future—especially since the newcomer himself has shown us new and unsuspected underground depths in all of us.*

*This Underground Man is dangerous because he carries the explosive charge of his freedom. Perhaps, though, it will also be the fault of the Crystal Palace if he has to stick pins into people in order to assert his freedom. And dangerous though he be, pins and all, he is certainly more interesting than the Crystal Palace itself, and we are likely to take his side against it since we too are human, like him, and cannot tolerate boredom very long. Since we are still living with him, still living him, our only recourse is to seek the least destructive and most valuable levels at which to release his aggressions, which can also become his freedom, since every act of freedom is an aggression against the void.*

*Now, for some 2500 years philosophers have been trying to build their own Crystal Palaces, in which this surd, this creature of shadow, would become as transparent as the walls of his geometrical hive. But the prolegomena to every future philosophy seems to be that it in turn will crumble and be superseded, that a philosophy is always less than the creature who produces it. Now a new step is being taken: it is proposed to place this creature with all his explosive liberty at the very center of philosophy itself. It will be interesting to see what comes of this.*

# Part 2

# HEIDEGGER:
# THE SILENT POWER
# OF THE POSSIBLE

Part 2

HEIDEGGER:

THE SILENT POWER

OF THE POSSIBLE

# I

## The Puzzle of Heidegger: The "Late" Heidegger

"THE NINETEENTH, the darkest of centuries," Heidegger says somewhere. I do not recall whether in that context he gives any reasons for this judgment. But we should not be hard put to find justification for it. If we think of two such opposed thinkers of that century as J. S. Mill and Nietzsche, their darkness seems to us at this distance as remarkable as their light: Mill, the saint of Utilitarianism, lost in the labyrinth of his own enlightened sophistries; and Nietzsche, blinded by the brilliance of his own vision, who was speaking of no one so much as himself when he cried, "We are unknown to ourselves, we knowers." To speak of that century as dark is not to deny it its greatness, to which Heidegger has elsewhere given ample testimony. But it leads us to ask: If the nineteenth is dark, what then of our own twentieth century? In a book on the philosopher Kant Heidegger concludes:

No other time has had so much and varied knowledge of man as ours. No other time has expressed its knowledge of man in so impressive and striking a way. No other time could supply this knowledge so quickly and easily. But on the other hand no other time knew less what man is than ours. Man has never become so questionable as in our time.

If then, in Heidegger's judgment, the nineteenth is the darkest, the twentieth would seem to be the most confused of centuries. Here too this judgment need not be taken to denigrate our century, whose historical task and greatness may be just to live through this confusion.

It may very well be said that Heidegger himself has added to this confusion. Among contemporary philosophers his influence begins to loom so large that he can no longer be dismissed out of hand, even by the most hostile critics. Yet even this influence has about it some of the perplexing character of the philosopher himself: operating in unexpected sectors of contemporary culture, it is on the other hand totally absent where one would think it ought to be operative. The greatest influence was undoubtedly in France, where Heidegger decisively shaped the thinking of the generation of Sartre and Merleau-Ponty; and yet these thinkers hardly followed Heidegger anywhere near to the end, and their thinking breaks off from his long before we reach the so-called "late" Heidegger. His influence has been strong in Italy, in Latin America, and Japan. Elsewhere not at all. So far as the world of Anglo-American philosophy is concerned, Heidegger has hardly made an entry at all; and what few fragments of his writings have come to the attention of philosophers have usually been greeted with sniggers of misunderstanding.

It may be that these philosophers are right, that the whole direction of Heidegger's thinking is mistaken, and his final achievement nugatory and worthless. But then he himself, with a kind of bold candor, has allowed for this possibility: the thinking he is engaged in, Heidegger tells us, is such that it can be in total error—not error that can be emended by qualifying this or that concept or argument; but error at the very root from which the thinking unfolds. Thought that takes upon itself the risk of going into the dark may end in darkness.

Part of the problem here is that the whole tradition of German philosophy itself is a very questionable one to current Anglo-American tastes. Some years back Bertrand Russell sounded the keynote for this fashion by declaring that Kant and Hegel were historical disasters. Perhaps; but then one would be hard put to understand the intellectual history of the West during the last two centuries apart from these "disasters." German philosophy is a very curious product of German culture, which in its turn cannot be understood apart from the strange history of that tormented nation, the most problematic of European peoples. It is hardly likely that a philosophy that is so characteristically a German expression would not also strike us as a very problematic thing. Heidegger places himself very boldly—and very radically—in the middle of this German tradition. Writing on Kant and Hegel, he maintains a dialogue with these dead philosophers as someone on the same footing. However arrogant such dialogue may seem, he restores these dead philosophers to a life they have in no other contemporary interpreter, so that he looks like their true heir and descendant—perhaps the last of that strange breed.

For those who have no taste at all for German philosophy, who find it an inflated subversion of "common sense," Heidegger with all the difficulties of his own philosophical idiom is not likely to be an appetizing dish. And here perhaps, as in most other matters, if you have no taste for a thing, better leave it alone.

But beyond the sectarian judgments of professional philosophers and the questionable character of German philosophy as a whole, the question of Heidegger seems to be implicated with the generally uncertain state of the culture of our time. The characteristic of avant-garde culture is that no reputations ever seem secure beyond question. Though the giants of the modern movement had seemed to establish themselves beyond question, time and again we are presented with revaluations of Joyce, Stravinsky, or Picasso that seek to recast the very foundations of our judgment of these creators. Perhaps this uncertainty must always attend the art of a revolutionary time. It is, of course, a cliché to speak of ours as a revolutionary age. The question is where does the revolution lie and in what does it consist. If revolution is taken as merely a highly accelerated rate of change, then we have not gone beyond a Sunday-supplement celebration of new plastics, transistor television, and rocket engines. The really revolutionary character of modern art does not lie in the sheer creation of novel forms, but in the fact that the artists have gone to the sources of their art and questioned its very premises. The revolution has broken the mold of tradition, but this destruction points toward new and unpredictable styles in art. In groping his way back to the very sources of his art the artist may even be left in that self-doubting mood that is expressed in the question of Arthur Honegger: "Have we indeed lost the arts?" It is natural then that the achievements of even the greatest contemporary artists should leave us doubtful of what they finally add up to because we cannot see the future they prepare.

Something of this uncertainty about the avant-garde infects one's judgment of Heidegger. It is also one of his fascinations for those who would like to see in philosophy some radical efforts to match the avant-garde achievements of contemporary art. Whether or not Heidegger is an equivalent in the domain of thought of a Joyce, Picasso, or early Stravinsky in their fields, is perhaps a futile, though teasing, question; but it is quite clear that like these artists he is seeking to break out of the mold of a tradition, and so seems to belong to our century in a way that few other philosophers do. If one compares him, for example, with Bertrand Russell, perhaps the most famous living philosopher, one is struck by the fact that in Russell the "modern" note is almost entirely lacking. Russell may make use of the modern devices of mathematical logic, but the context of all his thinking remains unchanged from that of Descartes and Hume. The effect is something like that of a composer who gives us a perfectly traditional tonal symphony slicked up with some streamlined orchestrations. Heidegger, on the other hand, is seeking to recast the context itself in which Western thinking has taken place since Descartes in the seventeenth century—and indeed, more ambitiously still, since the beginnings of Western thought among the ancient Greeks. So bold a venture of thought would imply that the thinker himself already stands outside this context.

One of the chief puzzles with the later Heidegger is just

how far outside this Western context he has stepped, or perhaps unwittingly strayed. This later phase can no longer be called philosophy in any academic sense. He is not doing philosophy, as our British cousins like to put it; he is *thinking*, as he himself calls it: attempting to stand open to the sources of Being rather than to fabricate an intricate conceptual structure.

Whether or not this kind of thinking has any use, or indeed any meaning—a question to be left unanswered at this point—it is quite clear that it differs from the whole tradition of Western philosophy.

In this connection there is an amusing and very revealing bit of dialogue between Heidegger and a Japanese in one of his most recent books, *On the Way Toward Language* (*Unterwege zur Sprache*), published in 1959. The title itself is characteristic of the later Heidegger, who is perpetually reminding us of the groping and tentative character of his thought: the book is not about the nature of language, as if Heidegger had this as an object securely in his grasp, but is only on the way toward sounding the depths of language. And the name of the interlocutor in the dialogue who is Heidegger himself is "the Questioner"—he who seeks but has not reached his goal.

The two speakers begin by recalling a dead friend, Count Kuki, who had been a student of Heidegger in years past. The Japanese tells Heidegger that after Kuki's return from Europe he had devoted himself to lectures on Japanese art and poetry, which he had attempted to explicate by means of Western aesthetics.

Heidegger immediately becomes suspicious and challenging: Did he have to do that? Did he have to turn to *aesthetics?*

But why not, replies the Japanese.

Because, Heidegger insists, aesthetics is something that has grown out of European thought, out of *philosophy*, and these must remain alien to the thought of the East.

The Japanese agrees that they are certainly alien but still the Easterner must make use of them.

But why, Heidegger persist, why must you have Western aesthetics?

Because, replies the Japanese, it may provide us with the necessary concepts for grasping our own art and poetry.

Must you have *concepts?*

Yes indeed, answers the Japanese, because since our contact with European thought we have become aware that our language lacks the power of conceptualization: the power to demarcate *objects* and relate them unambiguously one to another.

At this point one can almost hear the note of exasperation in Heidegger's voice: Do you seriously take that for a *lack* in your language?

And the conversation is launched from this point on as a search into the intricacies of Eastern and Western misunderstandings of each other.

What is most amusing and yet most significant in this brief exchange is that Heidegger, the Westerner, takes the side of the East against the whole apparatus of Western philosophy. Significant too, that the chief villain in the piece should be that branch of philosophy, aesthetics, which is the last ossified outgrowth from a conception of philosophy that was on its way to petrefaction. Aesthetics was established as a separate discipline within philosophy by Baumgarten only as late as the eighteenth century. Its *raison d'être* as a separate discipline was rooted in the traditional triad of the True, the Good, and the Beautiful; if logic and metaphysics dealt with truth, ethics with the good, then there must be a separate part of philosophy that would deal with the beautiful, and for this Baumgarten appropriated the word aesthetics, which derived from the Greek word for sense-perception. All this seems quite naturally, and indeed mechanically, rooted in the philosophic tradition; yet the remarkable thing is that this isolation of a distinct realm of the aesthetic had not been made before in Western thought, and that while the great philosophers from Plato onward had made searching analyses of art in one context or another, whether the context was political, ethical, metaphysical, or merely technical, it was always art within context, not art as a context to itself, distinct and *sui generis*.

It is not merely an historical accident that art, which was once discussed only contextually by philosophers, came to be treated as a separate sphere of experience known as the aesthetic. Nor did this change take place in the eighteenth century merely as a matter of conceptual thoroughness on Baumgarten's part, as if the great philosophers before him had not been tidy enough to follow out the consequences of their own classic triad of the True, the Good, and the Beautiful. No, the reason lies in the changed historical situation of art and of man's relation to art. For the Greek or the man of the Middle Ages, there could be no separate sphere of the aesthetic because that was not his experience of art. A Greek tragedy was the celebration of the presence and the mystery of the god, and the Greek audience, in the grip of that presence, could not behold the drama (literally, a thing done, a ritual) with the detached contemplation of the aesthete. The modern man of culture who witnesses a performance in New York of the medieval play of Daniel hardly has the experience of the man of the Middle Ages for whom this play, performed in a Cathedral, partook of the holy place and expressed the truth, not of aesthetic imagination, but the literal historical truth of holy writ. *The eighteenth century marks the development of the strictly modern institution of the museum.* It is no accident at all that museums should begin at a time when philosophers were elaborating a separate discipline of aesthetics; the two events flow from the same historical condition of man, in which from beginning to end all human thinking is rooted. In the museum we are in the role of the detached contemplator, the aesthetic subject, surveying works of art of the most heterogeneous kinds that have been detached from their original context of a church, a crypt, or the ancestral halls of a castle where the family portraits record the long line of ancestral blood backward to the earth. In the museum, no matter how subtle or refined our responses, we are spectators, and only dimly and by a stretch of the imagination, partakers of the presence that once surrounded and penetrated the work of art. In this sense we moderns are all "aesthetes," victims of aesthetics.

This changed relation to art, which is a profound fact in the *being* of modern man, naturally pervades his *thinking* about art, and hence shapes nearly all the aesthetic treatises of modern philosophers from Kant to Croce. They begin by seeking to mark out the distinct character of the aesthetic experience, as if cutting out a figure with scissors: *the* aesthetic experience is a state of disinterested interest, a judgment without a concept, an intuition as distinct from a concept, part of the theoretical rather than the practical moment of spirit, etc. etc. They start thus from the fact of consciousness, and their thinking never goes beyond the framework of philosophic subjectivism. It is perfectly in keeping with the nature of modern aesthetics that it was launched as a philosophic discipline in the Cartesian period of philosophy, after Descartes had grounded all philosophic thinking in the primacy of consciousness. On the one side is the mind, the conscious subject, on the other the object of consciousness. As soon as we use the term "the aesthetic experience," we have subtly committed ourselves to a way of thinking that places this consciousness on one side and the work of art as an object set over against it. We are operating from a dualism of subject and object.

Nothing could be further from the experience of art of the Orientals. For them the contemplation of the work of art transcends the subject-object dualism. The classic Chinese painter loses himself in the landscape until he has divested himself of all trammels of subjectivity, and then in the grip of the *Tao*, which is beyond the distinction of subject and object, spontaneously creates his painting. And the contemplator of the work of art is to repeat this process: he is to dwell with the work of art until he loses himself as contemplator, until he is no longer a subjective consciousness perceiving an object, until the unity of Being is no longer shattered by the artificial distinction between subject and object. To put it paradoxically; the Oriental believes that he has arrived at true aesthetic experience only when there is no longer such a thing as the aesthetic experience. The concepts of Western aesthetics, which speak in terms of a subjective consciousness, cannot illumine this unity of Being that transcends a purely subjective consciousness.

Heidegger's dissatisfaction with Western aesthetics must not be misunderstood here, no more than—as we shall see later—his rejection of Western "philosophy" generally. The efforts of Western aestheticians from Baumgarten onward have not been worthless: there have been essays in this field that match in brilliance anything achieved in other parts of modern philosophy, and there are those who hold, not without some justification, that Kant's work on aesthetics, the *Critique of Judgment*, is the greatest of his three great critiques. But as great as all the accomplishments of aesthetic theory may be, they take, in Heidegger's view, a false step when they start out from consciousness rather than Being, and so imprison their thinking within the framework of Cartesian subjectivism. That subjectivism, he feels, is the peculiar and baffling specter haunting modern thought; and his own thinking is an effort to prepare the way for a new and different historical epoch.

So too, his dissatisfaction with "philosophy"—and particularly with Western metaphysics—has nothing to do with the positivistic rejection of metaphysics. For the positivists, the whole of Western metaphysics is one huge grammatical mistake, the deception and self-deception practiced by philosophers who were victims of their own bad grammar and improper use of language. Though the motive for this judgment is a ruthless desire for clarity, the rejection looks almost as bleak and bald as Henry Ford's famous dictum that "History is the bunk." Heidegger's reverence for the past is too great to permit him any such act of *kultur-bolschewismus*. Philosophy, for him, is one of the very great things that the human spirit has accomplished. But the past is nevertheless the past, with all of the limitations of human finitude imprinted on it; and the task of the thinker who searches the past for its meaning is also to show the doors of possibilities that the tradition had closed.

This matter of history, and specifically the history of Western thought, we shall have to deal with more fully later. Suffice it for now if this fragment of conversation with a Japanese has pinpointed the fact that the thought of the late Heidegger moves beyond the tradition of the West, and consequently, like a good many other efforts of modern culture, places this tradition itself in question.

The dialogue was cited from a book, *On the Way Toward Language*, whose title reveals the philosopher's extraordinary preoccupation with the problem of language. At least this one interest unites Heidegger with a good many other contemporary and otherwise very divergent schools of philosophy. One of the hallmarks of twentieth-century philosophy has been a new and exhaustive preoccupation with the problem of language. But where this interest draws more positivistic-minded philosophers to examine only logic and science, it has taken Heidegger into the languages of poetry and art. Poetry, he holds, is not a mere ornament of culture, but the primary and essential form of language.

Hence, the thinker who exposes himself to poetry may gain through it some unique access to the meaning of Being. Since this last is the problem of problems for Heidegger, and since we are trying to gain some foothold for seeing his thought as a whole, it may be worthwhile to take a look now at some of his curious adventures with the poets.

# II

## Heidegger and the Poets

HEIDEGGER'S MOST MONUMENTAL WORK, *Sein und Zeit*
(*Being and Time*), published in 1927, made an immediate
and powerful impact upon the philosophic public. The
book seemed like a prelude to a grand new metaphysical
system, and philosophers expected subsequent works to
complete this system. Their expectation was heightened by
Heidegger's announcement that the published part of *Being
and Time* was only the first part of a projected work. When
would the second part appear? What would be the systematic results for philosophy after the humanly dramatic
and sensational analyses of *Being and Time*?

These expectations were never fulfilled: the second part
of *Being and Time* has never been published, and the very
nature of Heidegger's later thinking came to preclude any
possibility of a metaphysical system. Looking back now,
we can see the seeds of this dissolution of metaphysics in
*Being and Time*; yet a work that claimed to re-open for

modern philosophy the ancient question of the meaning of Being did quite properly seem to promise a new system of metaphysics: if the question were to be raised again, why not then eventually some comprehensive answer?

While the philosophical world waited in vain for such a system, Heidegger in the early 1930's turned instead to a study of poetry, particularly of the poet Hölderlin. The first essay on Hölderlin appeared in 1937, to be followed throughout the 1940's by a series of other studies of this poet. More recently Heidegger has published interpretations of Rilke, Gottfried Benn, Georg Trakl, and Stefan Georg. His concern with poetry, far from being a passing fad, has become a more consuming involvement over the years.

Quite a few philosophers greeted with suspicion this original adventure into the realm of poetry. Heidegger appeared to be laying aside the sober concern of philosophy in order to indulge himself in the sensuous and emotional luxuries of poetry. Nothing could be more traditional than this suspicion that thinking must lose its rigor if it deals with poetry and the poets. At the very dawn of Western philosophy Plato had relegated poetry to the realm of unreality in comparison with philosophy. This denigration of poetry is not Plato's personal pique against the poets of his time, but an inevitable consequence of the Platonic dualism between the world of intellect and the world of sensation, the former consisting of eternal ideas that are grasped by the intellect alone, the latter of the fleeting and changing data of the senses, with which the practicing artist is involved. Since that which endures, the eternal, is more valuable than that which is transitory, the temporal, the realm of ideas has a fuller reality than the world of sense. Hence all art, in opposition to pure science and rational philosophy, traffics in the shadowy and unreal world of the senses. This Platonic doctrine, sometimes more openly and sometimes in more subtle and hidden form, has infected the philosophic view of poetry since the beginning of Western thought. In another aspect, it constitutes the prejudice of traditional Western humanism for the strictly rational in man as against all other psychic functions.

But Heidegger's thought is nothing less than a rejection of Platonism in all its forms, perhaps the most stringent rejection among the many similar efforts in our apparently anti-Platonic time. Hence it should have been guessed that this anti-Platonism would carry with it an evaluation of poetry totally different from Plato's: far from dealing with a derivative or second-rate reality, poetry is essentially revelation. Nor is this revelation idle or trifling, for the fate of poetry in the modern period is involved in a unique way with the destiny of Western civilization. For Heidegger, every human reality, being temporal, is also historical; and modern poetry, as an historical reality, has raised the fundamental problem of man and his destiny in a startling form. This note of historical prophecy resounds in Hölderlin in its most extreme and uncanny form, and that is why Heidegger has singled him out as the poet of poets: the poet of poetry itself in the sense that he is involved with the very fate of poetry.

The poets tell us of a rather strange moment of history in which we are caught. We need not confine ourselves to the poets whom Heidegger interprets, since poets in our own tongue, whose words we can hear directly, may serve as more compelling witnesses.

For Yeats, perhaps the greatest poet in English in this century, ours is the time of the dark of the moon. The full moon, symbol of subjectivity and the contemplative wisdom that prevailed in former epochs, has vanished, and the dark of the moon is the time of empty and senseless extroversion, and so of empty and senseless violence too. "Violence upon the roads, violence of horses . . ."

For T. S. Eliot the modern world is the desert wasteland in which the healing waters do not flow. The sun beats down pitilessly and there is no rock to provide the shelter of shade, and no water. Our air is now "thoroughly small and dry/smaller and dryer than the will."

For Robert Graves our time is out of touch with "the lady of the house," the Great Goddess, and we have turned nature upside down by all kinds of capricious intellectual experiments. Trees are merely timber for sawmills, animals belong to the circus or the cannery, and even women, avatars of the Goddess, are "mere auxiliary state personnel." And the suffering poet must ask, "What is the use and function of poetry nowadays?" echoing the cry of Hölderlin more than a century earlier, "What use are poets in a needy time?"

No doubt, other poets could be cited who are more at ease in the contemporary Zion. But in these matters unanimity is not required; it is something to think about that a good number of modern poets, and among them some of the greatest, feel a deep historical anxiety about the way the world is going. No doubt too, your judgment of the value of the poets as witnesses will also depend on your basic view of what poetry is. Perhaps the poets are bound to be reactionaries because they are plying a trade that belonged to the ancient but has gone out of fashion in the modern world. The positivistic critic, I. A. Richards, has pointed out that the great bulk of poetry in the past was produced in connection with a "magical" view of the universe that modern science has dispelled; hence it is natural to expect that contemporary poets will not have severed the umbilical cord and will still hanker after the primordial tie of poetry with myth and magic. But the poet, Richards goes on, like everybody in the modern world must learn to *adjust:* he has to recognize that his place is no longer that of the seer, as it was once among ancient peoples, but merely that of a man skillful at manipulating words to stimulate our emotions and resolve these stimuli harmoniously for our own better *adjustment.*

On the other hand, if you tend to a more old-fashioned view of poetry, and if you have at all lived with and in the work of some poets, you are likely to believe still that a poet is a poet through his vision, that poetry is really revelatory, and accordingly you will take more seriously the poets as witnesses to their time. That is why this writer has cited poets (and the list could be extended) with whom he has lived enough to believe them as poets, and to believe them as poets is to take them seriously as historical witnesses. Their testimony corroborates the judgment Heidegger has drawn from his own list of German poets.

But no matter what your general view of poetry—as vision or as mere emotional contagion—this malaise of the poet in modern times is something to think about. To think about, not just to make the subject of literary prattle. Though this alienation of the modern poet has been talked about repeatedly, neither philosophers nor historians have thought about it deeply enough.

It is, after all, an historical phenomenon unique in the history of poetry. When did this phenomenon first appear? This question, at any rate, is not very difficult to answer: from the contemporary poets who are anxious about the modern age there is a direct line back through the nineteenth century to the beginnings of Romanticism. It is with Romanticism that this strange new chord of anxiety is sounded in literature. The English-speaking reader may take Blake and Wordsworth as clear examples. The anxiety here is that man has entered upon some new and uncertain turning point in his history in the course of which he will become severed from nature so that the voice of the poet will not be heard and poetry itself become a dead art of the past. This uneasy vision of the poets—we shall go into it more in detail later—already contains the main themes of Heidegger's philosophical view of history.

This uneasiness of the poets that begins with Romanticism, we have said, is an historically unique phenomenon. It is necessary to insist upon this point, because its meaning would be lost if we merely took it blandly that yes, of course, poets have quarreled with the contemporary world, but after all poets have always been quarreling with their times. "The irritable race of poets," as the Latin poet puts it. Yes, indeed, poets have quarreled with their times before, but there are quarrels and quarrels, and with Romanticism a very different kind of quarrel begins. No poet ever lashed at his society or his fellow citizens more savagely than

Dante against his native Florence and fellow Florentines. Yet this is the anger of a citizen who has been exiled for political differences, not of a poet who feels that he has been exiled through the sheer fact of being a poet. The anger of Aristophanes against Athenian politics and politicians is that of a citizen who has his place in the community as a poet. The Roman poets lamenting the decay of the times— as Horace bewailing the present generation as a decline from its forebears—are writing *political* odes, which means that the form itself assumes that the voice of poetry can be heard. If we come as far forward even as the neoclassicist Pope, his satire against his time is the voice of a poet who, as poet, still retains his place as a man within society.

The Romantic poet's quarrel with his time is something very different: it is the uneasiness that simply because he is a poet, insofar as he is a poet, he has been placed beyond the pale and cut off from the rest of mankind, who no longer listens to the poet's voice. This has happened because man has taken the prodigious historical step of severing himself from nature. For what is poetry but man's primordial celebration that he belongs to the earth?

Poet and thinker, says Heidegger, dwelling on mountain-peaks apart, are yet nearest of kin. As the Romantic poets seek to express the alienation of man from nature, so Heidegger's central theme as a philosopher is the severance of man from Being.

Now, among the Romantic poets Hölderlin is the most stark and extreme of the visionaries obsessed with this new historical theme, and that is why Heidegger chooses him as his central poet. Hölderlin is the poet of "the night of the world," this present stage to which history has brought us: the night from which all the gods have departed and where the god to be has not yet been born; the night in which man must stand in somber and lucid courage before Nothingness. So too, for Heidegger the philosopher, Nothingness is not a meaningless word, a mere negative concept, or a passing emotional vapor, but a real historical and philosophical problem that man faces now as never before in history.

# III

## Heidegger and the Poets (Continued)

HÖLDERLIN AND NIETZSCHE, the solitary poet and the solitary thinker, are the two dark angels that preside over the thought of the later Heidegger. These two, poet and thinker, are spiritually akin, and share the same destiny. Passionate Hellenists, dazzled by the light of Greece, they succumbed eventually to the darkness of psychosis. There is something archaic and awesome about their breakdowns, reminding us that earlier peoples spoke of insanity as "the sacred disease." Heidegger says eloquently of Hölderlin—and exactly the same might be said of Nietzsche: "He was received into the protective night of madness." There is something at once uncanny and holy about these tragic figures, who in the extremity of their destiny are symbols of all that is extreme and uncanny about the destiny of the Germans. Hölderlin speaks of "the wine-god's holy priests, who go from land to land to land in the holy night." The verse is apt for both himself and Nietzsche, priests of this "holy night" that is now both crisis and opportunity for man. In this sense both Hölderlin and Nietzsche are culture heroes, sacrificial victims for the rest of the tribe, if that remnant has at all the will to be saved.

Heidegger's involvement with Hölderlin, then, was no departure from philosophy but the entrance into his most real philosophic problems. But even apart from Hölderlin's themes, the philosophic quest of Heidegger would have led him to think about poetry. For the poet, he has said, gives voice to Being; and for Heidegger the alpha and omega of philosophy is the problem of Being.

Being? It is high time, in the course of these fumbling and tentative efforts to get our hooks into the leviathan, that we stop to justify this unpopular word. If it were unpopular only with the professional philosophers, that would not matter so much; but the word hardly strikes any interested response from the ordinary and literate person who hears it. Being—with a capital B—seems to transport us immediately into some abstract and rarefied region far above the mundane and concrete affairs of daily life. And the Problem of Being! That sounds like the last thing that would have anything to do with the real realities of death and taxes. And to make matters worse, the word itself is a very poor equivalent for Heidegger's word, *das Sein*. This latter is a verb—the infinitive of the verb "to be" in German— while "Being" in English, though it is formed from the participle of the verb, is taken as a noun when used separately. The difference between the noun and the verb is crucial here: a verb carries with it always a determination of tense (time), while a noun signifies some object apart from any reference to time. The noun cuts something out of the flux of time and fixes it as an essence for all eternity in some timeless realm of discourse. The task is to bring back into the word "Being" the sense and urgency of the temporal.

Perhaps some progress out of this verbal morass may be made by beginning with the humbler word "being" in lower case. Here is a word which, used as a noun, seems readily enough understood. Man is a being, so is a star, and this table too. Anything that is, is a being. The word means the same as "entity" or "thing"—this last taken in its most general sense. Thus it is a word of utmost generality, the common character of all things that are, and therefore almost indeterminate in connotation. Though we understand it readily enough, we do so by taking it as a functional and empty counter of discourse, more or less like the pronoun "it" whose meaning is one that we wait to fill out. Hence we should expect that traditional metaphysics, which as the science of being qua being aimed to tell what were the characteristics of all beings just insofar as they were beings, would yield no concrete and useful conclusions either for the positive sciences or for daily life. That kind of metaphysics was bound to be a sitting duck for positivistic criticism.

When we come now to the word "Being"—with a capital B—we have to venture upon a somewhat more irregular verbal maneuver. The suggestion is provided by Heidegger himself, and it is rather remarkable that none of his interpreters has seized upon this key passage, page 70 of his *Introduction to Metaphysics*:*

---

* Yale University Press.

We understand the verbal substantive "Being" [*Sein*] from the infinitive, which in turn remains related to the "is" in all its variety of forms. The definite and unique verbal form "is," *the third person singular of the present indicative*, takes precedence over all other forms. We understand "to be" [*sein*] not in relation to "thou art," "you are," "I am," or "they were," which are just as much part of the conjugation of "to be" as "is." "To be" [*sein*] is for us the infinitive of "is." Hence we interpret the infinitive "to be" [*sein*] from the "is."

"Being" is to be understood from the "is": the reader may take this as a bit of etymological pettifoggery, but it is, in fact, a point central to the whole of Heidegger's thought. In accordance with Heidegger's suggestion here, we may try as a translation for his phrase, *das Sein des Seiendes,* which is usually translated as "the Being of what-is," the following: the Is of what-is.

*The Is of what-is!* If the reader is patient enough to put up with this barbarism for a moment, it may help to clarify matters a bit.

First of all, this Is of what-is—in its sheer presence—is what poet and artist make manifest. People under the influence of mescalin have described the wonderful perceptions they have had of the most ordinary objects. The chair across the room, Aldous Huxley tells us, is not blurred or distorted, but remains just what it is, a chair, but a chair that shines now with its own Being. Without drugs we get a similar experience from art in Van Gogh's painting of a little wicker chair: IT IS, just that little chair, manifest and open to us; and the simple yet astonishing miracle is that it *is*.

Because this Is of what-is—the sheer presence of what is present—becomes obscured for us by the routines of practical living and the clichés of ordinary chatter, we need the poet to restore it to us. To surrender to poetry is to bring ourselves once again before this Is of what-is, the situation of wonder and astonishment with which thinking began among the earliest Greeks. Hence the hidden link between poet and thinker, as Heidegger sees it, since both start from the same root experience.

The verb "is" is in the present tense. "Present" here must be understood in two senses: (1) in the temporal sense, obviously, as that which is present in time; but also (2) what is present is before us, open and manifest, revealing itself. We have here two cardinal traits that attach to Being, as Heidegger understands it: first, the ineluctable temporal dimension of Being, and, secondly, the inseparability of Being from truth, which Heidegger understands in the sense of revelation, following the Greek *a-letheia*, literally un-hiddenness.

Nothing might seem more obvious and banal than these two meanings of "presence" extracted from the verb "is." But the obvious is sometimes what is most hidden to men when they begin to ratiocinate, and the profound thing about Heidegger is how radically he relates these two simple meanings to the whole tradition of Western thought. The title of his major work is *Being and Time*, and the collocation of these terms is no accident. If one thinks of that long tradition within Western philosophy from Plato through the Absolute Idealism of the nineteenth century, which denies that time is "really real" and relegates it to the realm of mere appearance, then the essential linking of time and Being appears as a radical revision of this tradition. Man longs for something stable amid the flux, and the intellect of philosophers, preferring a timeless world of essences, would also prefer as its ideal a language that contained only nouns and had eliminated verbs with their troubling references to tense. To make the verb resound within the traditional word "Being" is a step taken by a different kind of thinking.

Heidegger is equally radical in dealing with the sense of "true" involved in the verb "is." What is now present presents itself; hence there is no presence—no Is—without revelation, or truth. Hence truth is not a characteristic of a proposition, or a mind that makes the proposition, which is the traditional locus assigned to truth since Aristotle and which has inevitably led to all the devilish puzzles of subjectivism within modern philosophy; instead, truth is a characteristic of Being itself in the sense that in order for any fact to be *present* it must to some degree be revealed. The medieval philosophers spoke of Being and Truth as convertible—*Ens et verum convertuntur*—in the sense that a thing is truly what it is insofar as it measures up to the essence or form in God's mind: thus true gold conforms to the essence of gold, whereas false gold does not. Heidegger gives a very different twist to this old formula, which in fact is based upon an Aristotelian metaphysics of things or substances. Truth does not reside in the thing as an attribute in a substance; rather, truth is a condition for the presence of anything, which just insofar as it is present must have revealed itself. Truth, in the most basic sense, resides neither in the subject (the mind) nor the object (the thing), but in that enveloping presence within which the thing has already become present, or revealed. Unless there were such a presence we could never make true propositions about the thing. Thus truth, as a characteristic of mental judgments, has to be based on another and more primitive sense of truth. If this view looks very odd indeed to some philosophers, that may be because they are enclosed in a tradition beyond whose blinders they cannot see.

The Problem of Being, which sounds so portentous, has turned into the apparently much more humble question of the meaning of the word "is." So stated, the question may seem to be legitimate even for positivists and linguistic analysts. (If no word is intrinsically unanalyzable, why not then an analysis of the word "is"?) It would be a mistake, however, to think that the question, so simply put, can be just as simply answered by a tidy lexicographical analysis. The question has a way of spreading itself into other matters, and no simple listing of meanings will do. George Santayana wrote a very interesting little essay on the meanings of "is" some years back, but the full explication of the meanings later required the five volumes of his *Realms of Being*. And for Heidegger this little word has been the subject of a lifetime of meditation, leading him, as we have seen, into the language and rituals of poetry.

One or two points to bring this section to a close:

1) To ask about the meaning of "is" is not to inquire about any thing or object. The question is not, as traditionally put: What is the "really real" being or beings? Being is not to be located residually in any material substrate or substance, nor in any mental substance either. The question, in other words, is not about some thing or things

named by a noun, but about the meaning of a verb, and the most ordinary verb in the language at that.

2) This meaning is to be grasped as it reveals itself directly in all the encompassing presences of daily life.

3) Since the "is" remains irreducibly a verb, and therefore temporal in meaning, it carries the negative within itself, for the present opens out into the future that is not yet and the past that is no more. We say, for example: "Today *is* a perfect late summer day"; and in this "is" there is present the September that is not yet, and the departed summer that is no more. It is in this sense that Heidegger understands non-Being to be part of Being. You will not understand him on this point if you think of Being as some irreducible substrate whose solidity apparently includes no interstices of non-Being anywhere.

4) Finally: the primacy of the "is" for Heidegger over verbal forms like "I am" and "thou art" inevitably suggests a comparison with Martin Buber's famous concept of the I-Thou relation. According to Buber, I find reality only when I am able to say Thou to another person, and in so saying my own I is really born. For Heidegger, the I can meet the Thou only because *There is*—i.e., can meet only within some encompassing region of Being. After all, I have to meet thee *somewhere;* in relation to something, and in some context.

Buber speaks from a strictly human and personal point of view, Heidegger from the neutral point of view of the ontologist, the philosopher of Being. It is not at all that Buber is wrong here; from the human point of view he is undoubtedly right that we are real persons only if we have been able to meet another in the I-Thou relation. The difference between Heidegger and Buber here is not a simple matter of one right and the other wrong, but has to do with two very different kinds of "existentialism," and to this matter we now turn.

# IV

## The Two "Existentialisms"

So FAR WE HAVE proceeded rather irregularly from back to front, as it were, beginning with a few brief glimpses of the later Heidegger, the more cryptic and oracular thinker who has been carried beyond traditional Western philosophy into the primitive company of the bards. Now we have to reverse field, and follow out the steps by which his thought has been brought to this extremity.

Fortunately for us, there is very little biography to get hung up on. Heidegger has been a Professor, his life has followed the usual professorial stages of advancement, and whatever drama clings to him has been merely what has transpired in his thought. In this he differs markedly from existential philosophers like Kierkegaard and Nietzsche, whose lives may be singularly devoid of any great variety of *external* incidents or adventures but in whom we nevertheless always feel the individual person intensely and dramatically present behind and within the thought. It is the

difference, we shall see, between two kinds of "existentialists" and two kinds of "existentialisms."

Heidegger was born in 1889 in Messkirch in the Black
Forest region of Germany, and the only significant thing to
report about his early years was that he was raised as a
Catholic and destined for the priesthood, but quit the
seminary after he had lost his faith. It is incalculable what
mark this early experience may have left upon him, but it
is not usually the case that early indoctrination in Catholi-
cism recedes without leaving any traces. The present writer
does not know Heidegger personally, has never heard him
lecture, and exchanged only one perfunctory bit of correspondence with him. Yet on the one social occasion
when I met Mr. and Mrs. Paul Tillich, who knew Heidegger well, I ventured an impression of the man gathered
from his writings: "Heidegger strikes me as a South German Catholic who lost his faith and—remained a South
German Catholic"; and Mrs. Tillich, whose intuition of
people I found impressive, nodded enthusiastic agreement.
Such personal conjecture aside, the fact is that the early
exposure to medieval philosophy through his Catholic up-
bringing is a cardinal influence in Heidegger's thinking—an
influence very different but perhaps as significant as his passionate addiction to the Greeks and Greek philosophy. His
strict and plodding attachment to the obvious resembles
that of the great scholastics; and some of his brief later
essays have that peculiarly difficult but straightforward
simplicity of some of the *opuscula* of the medieval philosophers. Knowledge of the medieval philosophers as the great
connecting link between the Greeks and Descartes has been

essential to his unified grasp of the whole perspective of Western thought. One develops a different kind of insight if one comes to the moderns, like Descartes and Kant, from a primary exposure to medieval scholasticism.

In any case, it was with a book on a medieval philosopher —*Die Kategorien und Bedeutungslehre von Duns Scotus* (*The Theory of Categories and Meaning in Duns Scotus*) —that Heidegger made his philosophical debut in 1916. This book, to be sure, is hardly Heidegger come into his own: it is a straightforward scholarly analysis of a medieval *Speculative Grammar* that was once attributed to Duns Scotus but has now been determined by scholars to be the work of a member of the Scotist school, Thomas of Erfurt. Yet this work is not without bearing on the whole of Heidegger's career, for here at the very beginning, in this analysis of a metaphysical grammar, he is involved in the problems of language and Being that have been his unceasing preoccupation in the years beyond. And in the details of this Ph.D. thesis there are more than a few hints of the Heidegger to come, particularly in the analysis of the difference between noun and verb, which is a central point in Thomas of Erfurt's *Grammar*. This medieval treatise, moreover, is in itself of no small philosophical significance, and it is interesting to recall that it was one of the important influences upon Charles Sanders Peirce, the great American pragmatist, in his researches into semantics.

After this first quite unsensational thesis, the next step forward is a giant step indeed: the publication of *Being and Time* in 1927, which was something of a bombshell in the German philosophical world. Between this work and the earlier thesis there lies the great and shaping influence of Edmund Husserl, at that time the leading German philosopher.

*Being and Time* is dedicated to Husserl "in friendship and reverence," and in the book itself Heidegger acknowledges in a footnote how much he owes particularly to some of the unpublished writings of his teacher. Since some of these writings have been published, we have come to know how much indeed Heidegger did owe to Husserl. This dedication is a touching sign of the close personal relations between master and disciple. The relation was to become clouded in the years to come, and it has been even more clouded by gossip and misrepresentation of what actually occurred. The real story has not been and perhaps never will be told because of the reticence of the parties involved. Even on the philosophical level, the intellectual relation between the two, though it has been discussed repeatedly, has not often been treated justly. Heidegger could not have taken the step he did without the long and detailed analyses of Husserl that paved the way; but on the other hand at the very moment when he was most under the influence of Husserl, Heidegger's was a very different mind and very much his own. To ignore the debt to Husserl is to ignore all the analytic details that make Heidegger's own position more cogent; to dwell on this debt overmuch is to miss the point that the very terms of Husserl's thinking shut him off from the next step forward that Heidegger was to take. Husserl, the founder of phenomenology, like Moses showed the way toward the Promised Land but could not enter it himself.

Husserl had founded phenomenology as a way out of the

impasse in which philosophy found itself at the close of the last century, torn between the claims of idealists on the one hand and materialists, or realists, on the other. Husserl proposed phenomenology as a "third way"—a way that might lead out of the impasse. Idealism and materialism were speculative philosophies that made a metaphysical leap from experience to an all-embracing hypothesis about the ultimate nature of reality. Instead of this speculative leap, Husserl proposed that philosophy turn its eyes to see what was really given in experience and make an attempt to describe it purely, without preconceptions. This effort in pure description, without any preconceived hypotheses or falsifying abstractions, was to be phenomenology: a philosophical discipline that promised a fresh look at things, and Husserl's great rallying cry, "To the things themselves!," was to become a famous slogan for a whole generation of younger philosophers.

Among other things, phenomenology meant a fresh look at consciousness itself. Eventually it would lead to doubt whether anything like consciousness existed, at least as it had been traditionally spoken of by philosophers; and finally, with Heidegger, the term is discarded altogether.

In taking his point of departure from the pure data of consciousness, Husserl likened his own method to that of Descartes. In actual fact, though, Husserl's employment of the Cartesian method was to destroy the Cartesian theory of consciousness. Descartes had interpreted mind and matter as two substances, really distinct in the medieval sense of real distinction, with a very uncertain and mysterious point of intersection. Matter was extended substance—that is, stuff that filled space; mind an immaterial, or mental, substance, in which thoughts, ideas, and feelings "inhered" in some sense analogous to the way in which physical qualities, like color and shape, inhere in a physical substance. On the other hand, since mind was a radically different kind of substance from matter, an idea is present in the mind in an altogether different way from that in which a color or shape is present in a piece of matter. Obviously, to talk about consciousness in this fashion leads to all kinds of philosophical puzzles, and philosophers after Descartes were to be plagued by them.

Descartes is usually construed as the villain in the piece, but in fact he did not originate but merely fell victim to the traditional mode of speech about consciousness. This tradition goes back to Aristotle, significantly, not to Aristotle's work on psychology, from which philosophers might have derived an altogether different view of consciousness and its relation to the body, but to the Aristotelian logic. In his *Categories*, which is the first part of his logic, Aristotle distinguishes between the two expressions: "to be predicated of," and "to be present in." When we say, "Socrates is a man," the term "man" is predicated of "Socrates" because everything implied by the term "man"—such as the fact that man is an animal—is intended to be asserted of Socrates. But when we say, "Socrates is white," we do not intend to assert of Socrates everything that white is—such as that Socrates is a color. Socrates is said to be white in the sense that the color is *present in* his skin. The distinction is thus very obvious, and one that is altogether appropriate for ordinary language. The difficulty begins when we extend the distinction to mental entities, like ideas. When I have an idea, it is obvious that neither I nor my mind are that idea, and so "idea" is not something predicated of me or my mind. It must, therefore, be "present in" the mind. And this, again, is perfectly appropriate for ordinary language, for we do say quite commonly that an idea is in our minds. But what will do for ordinary language will not necessarily do for philosophic understanding. Indeed to the degree that we become habituated to a certain common mode of speech our concepts of the things intended may become twisted in order to fit that pattern of speech. Ordinary language may be inauthentic as well as authentic —a point that does not seem to have been observed by those contemporary British philosophers who would make ordinary language an absolute arbiter in all cases.

The Husserlian phenomenology, a summons to sweep away all obscuring language, brings a fresh look at mind itself. What does it mean for anything to be in my mind? That it is an object of which I am conscious. Consciousness is never without its correlated object; it is always consciousness *of*. . . . Husserl calls this the intentional aspect of consciousness: i.e., consciousness always intends an object beyond itself. Thus it is the very essence of consciousness to refer to a world beyond itself. Consciousness is not that hermetically sealed chamber that Descartes imagined, where ideas may be present from which a world outside may only doubtfully be inferred. A world is not something inferred at all: it is a structural component of all consciousness. What is given to me in direct experience is not a mind with ideas inhering in it, but rather a world with indefinite horizons, now contracting now expanding, in which things and people, close at hand or far off, remote in time or present, appear, persist, or disappear.

This elaboration of the idea of "world" as a structural component of all consciousness was the great achievement of Husserl's last period. The next step was Heidegger's: to dispense with the term "consciousness," and speak instead of man as fundamentally and essentially Being-in-the-world.

Man is thus not fundamentally a consciousness aware of objects. Before this, deeper than this, he is a being en-meshed in the world with its multiple possibilities in the total context of which he forges ideas as projects for ad-ministering things and shaping his own life. (The similar-ity here to certain strains in the pragmatism of William James and John Dewey is striking; the eventual differences, however, between Heidegger and these two great prag-matists are just as striking and perhaps even more signifi-cant.)

Such was the radical point of departure of *Being and Time*. Its basic insight into human existence is only begin-ning now to percolate into psychology. Though the book had an immediate impact at the time of its publication, the response tended to be colored too much by some of the more dramatic and sensational materials that Heidegger dealt with. (We have treated some of these matters in the first half of this book, and we need not now go into a more de-tailed itemization of the book's contents.) Heidegger may have had great psychological insight, as some of his severest philosophical critics were ready to concede, but that insight is not the heart of the matter: *Being and Time* is not a work in literary psychology, not a disguised confession or lyric, but a philosophical work. And its philosophical character has now to be shown by a link with the philosophical tradition far more significant even than the derivation from Husserl: namely, the relation of Heidegger's thought to Kant. It is the influence of Kant, more than Kierkegaard, that supplies the key to what is philosophically at issue in *Being and Time*, and that justifies our speaking of "the two existentialisms."

Heidegger had been quite emphatic at the beginning of *Being and Time* in announcing that his real problem was the problem of Being in general, and that his attempt to describe certain general structures of human existence was undertaken in order to find some clues to the more general problem. This word of warning fell on deaf ears in the case of some critics, perhaps because they had already a preconception of existential philosophy as fundamentally a dialectical lyric, an expression of the human pathos of the finite and striving individual. Their conception of existential philosophy, in short, revolved around Kierkegaard.

But in fact the points of view of Kierkegaard and Heidegger are diametrically opposed. This does not mean that they contradict each other, but simply that they are doing very different things. Kierkegaard is not an ontologist who is attempting to describe the general structures of human existence. If he does happen to make clear such structures, as notably in *The Concept of Dread* and *The Sickness unto Death*, it is incidental to his main purpose, which is religious. Where he touches upon the problem of human existence, it is to insist that this existence, which is irreducibly mine, can never be exhausted by any concept or system of concepts. This is the point of his famous polemic against Hegel in the *Concluding Unscientific Postscript*, where he insists that thought and existence can never be identical. The living individual, incomplete and changing, can never be swallowed up in any complete and static system. Man, as Karl Jaspers puts it, is always more than the sum of his thoughts—and cannot, we may add, be summed up in the thoughts of any behavioral scientist.

Kierkegaard is talking about the *actual* existing individual. Thought deals with universals, or *possibilities*, but the existence that we have to live, and not merely think, is one of gritty *actuality*. The speculative philosopher may deal with sheer possibilities as if he were, in Plato's words, a spectator of all time and existence. This is the attitude of detached contemplation, the attitude of the aesthete, as Kierkegaard calls it. But in life, as we live it, we cannot sit as mere spectators: we have to be involved, and as soon as we have made the decision of involvement, we have passed from a purely aesthetic to an ethical stage. In so doing, we become, as the common phrase puts it, a *real* person: we have put off childish things and become serious. "Reality" for Kierkegaard is not a highfalutin metaphysical problem at all: it has to do simply with the seriousness of the existing individual who has become real by committing himself to some ethical and religious decision.

Certain key points emerge from this Kierkegaardian treatment of existence:

1) Actuality is prior to possibility. Life is not an affair of hypotheticals and contrapositives, but of actual situations. I might have loved any number of other women, but the fact is that I love this woman and the hypotheticals vanish like vapors before this actual enmeshment.

2) The point of view on human existence is not that of

the philosophical theorist, but of the ethical and religious teacher who seeks to summon other individuals to the task of becoming a self. In this sense Kierkegaard refers to Socrates as his model and hero: not Socrates the dialectician but Socrates the human gadfly who sought to sting his fellow Athenians into following the only life that is worth living by a man. Philosophy here is not primarily a doctrine, but rather an appeal and summons to achieve an authentic life.

3) Kierkegaard's treatment of existence does not deal at all with the strictly philosophical problem of "transcendence" that has bedeviled modern philosophy since Descartes: the problem of how man, circumscribed in time and space, can nevertheless comprehend a world beyond himself.

On all of these three points exactly the opposite, as we shall see, has to be said for Heidegger.

Kierkegaard's treatment of human existence really turns on the traditional problem of universals and particulars. And his conclusion, if we may transpose it into more general and traditional language, is that the individual cannot be reduced to any mere nexus or set of universals. This is a traditional position that goes back to Aristotle. Kierkegaard's contribution is to dramatize the human discrepancy between the universal and particular that makes up the pathos of life itself—the discrepancy between the law and the individual case, between moral obligation and individual need, between the abstract psychological explanation and the individual mystery that we ourselves are.

His insistence that actuality is prior to possibility is equally traditional and Aristotelian, having come down through medieval philosophy in the form of the scholastic axiom: "*Actus prius ac melius est quam potentia.*" (Actuality is prior and higher than potentiality.) According to the Aristotelian view, possibilities, or potentialities, exist only because there are actual entities with certain actual structures or characteristics that can operate in a certain way. For example, I can walk—walking is a possibility for me—because I do actually exist and do have an actual pair of legs that function. The Aristotelian position here is simply the lucid expression of common sense insofar as it takes its cue from things or objects and regards potentialities as characteristic of things.

This traditional character of Kierkegaard's views leads Heidegger to say that Kierkegaard is no "thinker"—in the sense in which Heidegger himself is a thinker seeking to recast the traditional understanding of Being—but a religious writer; and, further, that Kierkegaard's ontology, as ontology, never went beyond what he had learned from Trendelenburg's commentaries on Aristotle. Heidegger does not mean to denigrate Kierkegaard by these remarks, but rather to indicate the limitations that really define his greatness.

Heidegger, on the contrary, is not a religious writer, and his philosophy is neither appeal nor exhortation but the strictly philosophical meditation of a thinker seeking to recast the meaning of the fundamental terms of Western metaphysics. How untraditional his thought is in comparison with Kierkegaard's can be seen in his reversal of the dictum that actuality is prior to possibility. At the very beginning of *Being and Time* he tells us: possibility is higher than (prior to) actuality. Man is a creature whose being is constituted by possibilities. Human existence cannot be understood from actual objects, but only from possibilities which, immediately and as such, make that existence what it is.

Can this be so? Can any actual entity be essentially constituted by possibilities? The traditional metaphysics, as well as common sense, says no: possibilities belong to a thing because of the actual structure and configuration of its parts. (This glass before me, for example, is break*able* because of the *actual* structure of its molecules.) The traditional metaphysics, as well as common sense, is a metaphysics of beings, or things, and so must speak in this way.

To see if there is any justification for Heidegger here we have to go back to Kant and the peculiar nature of the inquiry that Kant was conducting in the *Critique of Pure Reason*. The Kantian *Critique* is not a treatise in psychology although Kant is analyzing the nature of mind in order to establish the certainty and the limits of human knowledge. Kant distinguishes between an "empirical" and a "transcendental" inquiry. An empirical inquiry examines individual facts or events in order to find the laws that govern these facts or events. Psychology, as an empirical science, attempts to do just this. A "transcendental" inquiry, however, which is what Kant is pursuing in the *Critique*, seeks to find the a priori conditions without which there could be no experience of particular facts or events. For example, the necessary condition for my perceiving any individual spatial entity is that space itself be given as a context within which that entity is perceived. Space, as the form of perception, provides the very possibility for any perception of an individual spatial entity. The intent of Kant's analysis here was to correct the psychological atomism of David

Hume, who had attempted to exhibit all the objects in experience as complexes of elementary "impressions"—or sense-data, in the more modern jargon. Thus space—or at least visual space—would be constructed as an aggregate, or set, of colored patches, i.e., individual spatial entities. Kant contends, on the contrary, that we are able to perceive a colored surface spread out in space only within an environing spatial context. The patch of wall across the room, for example, is perceived within a larger environing spatial context. For certain mathematical purposes three-dimensional space may be regarded as an aggregate of points; but quite obviously this is not the way space is given in experience: I can see a small dot only as it occurs within a larger plane. The Kantian analysis, in contrast to the atomism of Hume, is holistic and contextual throughout. Every individual fact or event occurs within a context, and this context must always be presupposed as the very possibility for the occurrence of that fact or event. Thus from the Kantian point of view possibility is prior to actuality: every individual experience occurs within a context that makes it possible.

Heidegger in *Being and Time* is pursuing just such a transcendental inquiry as Kant's although the fundamental terms of the inquiry have been transposed from consciousness to Being. Heidegger, in short, is asking what are the general and a priori conditions that make possible certain individual facts of human existence. These conditions, as the possibilities for any individual mode of human existence, must be given as the context within which the individual events of our existence occur; and this is the sense in which Heidegger asserts that possibility is prior to actuality. As

Kant distinguished between the empirical and the transcendental, so Heidegger makes a parallel distinction between "ontic" and "ontological." An ontic inquiry is concerned with individual and *actual* facts or events, and seeks to establish some general classifications and laws for these actualities; an ontological inquiry is concerned with the general structures that, as potentialities, pervade human existence.

This distinction between the ontic and ontological is cardinal for the understanding of Heidegger, and yet it is remarkable how many of his critics have missed its implications. Consequently, they fail to see that the key terms of Heidegger's analysis—Being-in-the-world, care, anxiety, death, guilt, moods (*Stimmungen*)—name possibilities and not actual occurrences or attitudes. Thus death, as Heidegger uses the word, does not mean the actual event of dying, decease; rather, it is a possibility—the possibility not-to-be—that pervades human existence. As such a possibility, it forms the temporal context, or horizon, of my finitude; and it is only within such a context that I can make any actual decision about my own personal attitude (an ontic fact) toward death. Sartre, as well as other critics who have taken issue with Heidegger's notion of human existence as a Being-toward-death, miss this point. Heidegger's view is not refuted by the fact that some men actually do long for death or have the ecstatic self-surrender to it of a Japanese *kamikaze* pilot. For such individual decisions about one's attitude toward death can be made only on the basis and within the context of one's own possibility not-to-be—that is, only as this possibility has been revealed as constitutive of one's own existence. Sartre, indeed, moves back and forth perpetually between the ontic and the ontological levels without ever seeming to be aware of their difference.

Similarly, Being-in-the-world is not intended to cover the actual facts of one's involvement with the world: one's cares as a citizen, parent, friend, and the rest. All of these matters are real and earnest, and they should long ago have carried human weight with those philosophers who wanted a proof of a world external to consciousness. But these individual concerns are possible only to a being who is already within the world: that is, to a being whose very essence is to be beyond himself within a world.

So too with all the other key terms in the Heideggerian analysis: they do not name ontic facts—individual attitudes or decisions—but ontological structures—i.e., possibilities that, as possibilities, constitute the very nature of human existence. Man is a creature of possibilities: *ein Wesen der ferne*, as Heidegger calls him, a creature of distance. Existence means *ek-sistenz*—i.e., literally, the standing outside himself. Man's existence is not riveted to the immediate moment in time, or his immediate surrounding habitat in space, like the animal: his being, immediately and as such, is spread out temporally and spatially into distant regions beyond himself. Man transcends himself; more accurately, he is a transcendence. And transcendence is an essential part of his nature because he is a being whose actual existence is constituted by possibilities. Hence the sense of Heidegger's emphasis that possibility is higher than actuality; and hence too the necessity of his reversing the traditional Aristotelian and scholastic dictum that the actual is prior to the possible.

The problem of transcendence became acute for philosophers with the beginning of modern physics in the seventeenth century. As soon as nature had been construed in the strictly mechanical terms of mass and extension, the question arose how all the other qualities of matter that consciousness perceives originated, and indeed how any state of consciousness itself could arise from the motions of material particles. If I look around me now, my consciousness is in immediate possession of a visual field beyond myself. Within this field there is a variety of shapes, textures, colors; and these colors appear quite naturally spread out on the surfaces of things. But if I try to think how this happens in purely mechanical or physical terms, I encounter abysmal mystery. I turn my glance, for example, to the opposite wall and I see a light-brown panelled surface; nothing would seem more simple and immediate, yet if I think of this as a physical chain of events, it becomes enormously complex. This chain begins with the wall's emitting certain particles of energy that strike my eye, and these impulses are transmitted through the optic nerve to the brain; then this impulse of energy—or commotion of particles, depending on what physical theory you start from—is transformed into a conscious state; and this conscious state projects a colored surface at a distance. But this last is a mystery: How can a physical state, localized in the brain, *transcend* itself and "project" a color (which does not really exist in the physical world) at a distance?

This is not the place to run through all the twistings and turnings of philosophers since Descartes in an effort to answer this question. What emerges from three centuries of struggle with the problem is this: the fact of transcendence cannot be derived from physical events where nothing like transcendence is present. Wherever this is attempted we do not get any solution essentially better than the naive explanation of the materialist Hobbes: that the "projection" of qualities on to things takes place because the atoms that make up the eye, or other sensoria, resist the impact of the oncoming atoms flowing from the object, and so generate a motion outward. If this sounds naive, it has on the other hand the virtues of candor and simplicity, and exhibits its weaknesses more directly than other more complex solutions. If, then, transcendence cannot be a derived, it must be a primitive fact. That is, the fact of transcendence must be as basic a fact as the existence of solid bodies bound by their own surfaces. And this, of course, is the way it is actually given in experience: there are not just bodies around me and my own consciousness which perceives them, but the enveloping presence within which bodies and consciousness are both present.

The difficulties that philosophers have had with the fact of transcendence are due to the fallacy of locating the existence of a thing strictly within its boundaries. The philosopher Whitehead aptly baptized this "the fallacy of simple location": the fallacy of common sense that a thing is located just where it is, i.e., confined to its own skin. Whitehead locates the traditional source of this fallacy in the Aristotelian doctrine of "primary substance." A primary substance, for Aristotle, is a concrete individual thing, this chair or this table, in which qualities and attributes inhere. Primary substances are thus the ultimate supposita of reality. With the development of the new physics in the modern period Aristotle's primary substances become transformed into material substances: bits of stuff extended in space. And there the difficulties with transcendence become acute.

This is as far as Whitehead takes the problem historically. Heidegger carries the historical interpretation from Aristotle's theory of primary substance back to the way in which the Greeks posed the problem of Being itself. Instead of sticking with the question, what is Being?, in the sense of, what is the Is?, the Greeks replaced this by the question, what are the things-which-are? They forgot the verb in Being and asked only after the noun. Thus the question of Being became transformed into the question of reality, and reality is always an object of some kind or other. Plato in his *Republic* makes the question of questions: What is really real? And the "really real" things he takes to be the eternal objects, the Ideas. Aristotle brings Plato down to earth and takes as the "really real" things the primary substances; concrete individual things. Being as the Is, as the enveloping presence within which things stand forth and are revealed, is forgotten. When things alone are real, then transcendence becomes a purely "subjective" phenomenon, a curious quirk of the human mind, something altogether unique and inexplicable in a world of things. Hence Heidegger's contention, which is borne out by the whole history of modern philosophy, that the problem of human transcendence can be adequately met only if we go back to the question of Being and pose this question in a radically different way from that of the tradition.

The transcendence we have been talking about is not the kind of transcendence that is dealt with by Kierkegaard, Nietzsche, or in this century Karl Jaspers. In these existentialists the problem of transcendence has to do with the developing individual's overcoming of himself in order to become authentically himself. To transcend oneself in this sense is a thoroughly personal act that can never be taught by any universal rule but that each of us has to live out for himself in fear and trembling. "Do not follow me," Nietzsche's Zarathustra remarks to some of his would-be followers, "Follow yourself." Because it is something that has to be lived, this task of self-overcoming is one of utmost seriousness requiring the commitment of ethical and religious decision, even where this religious decision may be, as in the case of Nietzsche, for atheism. As a uniquely individual task, moreover, it falls outside the theoretical purview of philosophy. That is why so many academic philosophers, who are aware only of this kind of existentialist, think of existentialism as something that has no relevance to the proper problems of philosophy at all. From the point of view of the existentialist task and its urgency, on the other hand, the orthodox problems of philosophy may strike us as mere mandarin's pastimes. In the grip of anxiety, or merely as we are involved in the daily struggle for a decent human happiness, we are likely at moments to feel that the whole of philosophy, as Pascal said of it, "is not worth half an hour's time." The overwhelming task for existentialists like Kierkegaard or Nietzsche can be put into one question: How do I become an individual? This is one kind, but only one kind, of existentialism.

Transcendence, as this uniquely human task, is an ontic

fact. That is, it is an actual development undergone by some actual human beings. The transcendence that Heidegger is talking about, however, is an ontological structure: it is existence itself taken as *ek-sistenz*, the standing outside itself. Only because man, insofar as he is man, stands beyond himself, *can* he engage himself in any actual (i.e., ontic) struggle to transcend himself. Here, once again, the ontological provides the possibility of the ontic. Or, in more common lingo, every fact is possible only within a context.

It is this distinction, then, between the "ontic" and the "ontological" that provides the key for distinguishing the two basic forms of existentialism. There is the existentialism that goes back to Kierkegaard, and past him to Pascal, and even to the *Confessions* of St. Augustine. It moves on the ontic level, and is fundamentally concerned with the salvation of the individual. Nietzsche partly belongs in this tradition insofar as his primary problem is also the salvation of the individual, naturalistically understood; but there is also the other side of Nietzsche that is forgotten for his literary brilliance: Nietzsche the systematic thinker—as much a systematic thinker, says Heidegger, as Aristotle. And indeed it is to some of the later studies of Heidegger that we are indebted for making clear the extent to which Nietzsche's thought is involved systematically with the whole history of Western metaphysics.

Karl Jaspers, by his very conception of philosophy as an *appeal* to authentic selfhood, places his thinking on the level of the ontic.

Only Heidegger sticks strictly to the ontological level. This does not at all mean that he is greater than these other existentialists, only that he is doing a different kind of thing

and sticks more consistently to his point of view. It is because he is not concerned as a thinker with ethical persua-
sion or exhortation that he made the simple statement in
1947 that has created misunderstanding in many minds, "I
am not an existentialist." At the time, of course, he was
particularly concerned with separating himself from the
existentialism of Sartre, which was then at the height of its
boom in Paris.

Sartre indeed is rather the extreme case of the existentialist shuttling between the ontic and ontological points of
view. In his *Being and Nothingness* he sets out as an ontologist attempting to give a phenomenological description
of Being, employing for that purpose all the apparatus of
Heidegger and Husserl; yet at the most crucial points he
slips back to the level of the ontic. Perhaps this confusion is
inevitable in a man whose thinking has been so vigorously
programmatic as leader of a literary school and in a way a
moral leader of his generation in France, and whose thought
is therefore addressed as an appeal and summons to other
free individuals.

The difference between Sartre and Heidegger comes out
nowhere more sharply than in their different points of view
on acts and potentialities. Sartre's dictum, "You are your
life"—with its correlate, "Your life is nothing but the totality of its acts"—is the expression of a moralist warning
us that when the final account of any individual life is cast
up there is no evasion from the responsibility of just what
that individual has done and left undone. We can find no
solace in the might-have-been. Possibilities that have not
been actualized are empty and unreal. "Man is what he

does," as André Malraux put it almost a generation earlier; and Sartre's philosophy is a detailed and lengthy elaboration of Malraux's summons to adventure. For Sartre, Doing takes precedence over Being, and the will to action becomes the central feature of man. Thus he ends in diametrical opposition to Heidegger, who denies both these contentions. Sartre is talking on the ontic level—the level of individual acts and actualities—not on the ontological level that sees existence as essentially constituted by its possibilities. From this latter point of view, which is Heidegger's, Being must take precedence over Doing, since every significant human action must take place within some context that already *is*. And the will to action, this celebrated banner of the modern epoch, must, if it is not to be blind and violent in its exercise, let itself be guided by things as they are. The will to action, if it is to be humanly significant, must at some point let-be: that is, it must let the truth of things manifest itself in order to direct its own exertions.

No doubt, the existentialists of the "ontic" variety tend to have a greater human appeal. They have the note of urgency and passion; and in addressing their appeal to the individual to become who he is, they speak to us as concrete men of flesh and blood. In comparison with their passion, Heidegger's ontological analysis may seem somewhat bleak and chilly. And because this ontology is ethically neutral, he himself has been accused more than once of moral nihilism. The Heideggerian *Dasein*, it has been charged, does not give us the concrete man of flesh and blood. Perhaps. But the criticism has as much point as an objection to Kant that his *Critique of Pure Reason* does not give us the living breathing human individual.

Yet the Heideggerian conception of human existence as a field of possibilities is not without its own grandeur. "The silent power of the possible," one of his most telling phrases, is the keynote to his thought and that is why we have chosen it as a title for this essay. This silent power is always at work in man; it ensures that the doors of the future are never completely closed upon him, however much he may have boxed himself in his contemporary historical situation. This silent power of the possible must be remembered in the face of some later pronouncements by Heidegger on Western history that seem to seal the doom of this civilization. Even here, as we shall see, at his gloomiest he does not close the door of the future upon man.*

---

\* It is rather ironical that this phrase, "the silent power of the possible" (*die stille Kraft des Möglichen*), was singled out by Sartre himself and used in a memorable essay on William Faulkner's *The Sound and the Fury*. Sartre criticizes Faulkner for sealing off his characters in a kind of doom-enclosed world without any doors open upon the future. Faulkner forgets, says Sartre, "the silent power of the possible" that is always at work in man. The criticism is that of a humanist and moralist. The irony is that the point that Sartre has perceived on a humanistic and moral level he lets slip away from him as an ontologist.

# V

## Heidegger and Kant

In 1929, two years after the publication of *Being and Time*, Heidegger succeeded to the chair of philosophy at the University of Freiburg from which Husserl had just retired. The relations between the two men were still cordial. Because of the prestige with which Husserl had endowed it, the chair at Freiburg was then the most important in Germany. Heidegger had arrived, his position in the official world of academic philosophy was secure; and as if in celebration, he published in the same year three important works: a book, *Kant and the Problem of Metaphysics*, and two shorter essays, *What is Metaphysics?* and *On the Nature of Cause*.

These last two works, and particularly the essay on cause, mark the turning point in Heidegger's thought. This was not perceptible at the time, not even to Heidegger himself, who had still to take a considerable step before arriving at the stage of his later thought. Because this turning point is so significant for the understanding of Heidegger's development, we defer discussion of these two essays to the next section and confine ourselves here to the book on Kant.

Heidegger's interpretation of Kant is one of his most powerful, incisive, and at the same time controversial productions. It bothers Kantian scholars by the boldness and simplicity with which it transports Kant's problems into the domain of Heidegger's own thinking. But this procedure is deliberate and not the forgetful oversight of a tyro. Heidegger is a philosopher maintaining a dialogue with another philosopher, not a doxographer producing a tidy compendium designed to help some student through a Ph.D. examination on Kant. Scholars can at times be very shortsighted people; and in this case they need to be reminded of Hegel's statement that the true history of philosophy is itself philosophy and not a parroting of opinions. A past philosophy comes to life only in the dialogue with another real philosopher. The question is not whether Heidegger distorts Kant by translating the latter into his own language, but whether this collision of minds strikes any spark of real philosophical insight.

We shall not attempt here to repeat the contents of this book step by step. That would take us too far afield into matters of special interpretation. We shall content ourselves with the central line of the book's argument as another essential link between the Kantian and Heideggerian mode of thought. Our last chapter dealt with the link between Kant and Heidegger on the question of possibility and actuality; here the link has to do with the essential temporality of man —a Heideggerian position toward which Kant himself was groping.

One of Kant's aims in writing the *Critique of Pure Reason* was to justify the certainty of human knowledge against the skepticism of David Hume. For Kant this took the form of the question: How are synthetic judgments a priori possible? In order to be necessary and certain these judgments would have to be a priori rather than a posteriori, prior rather than posterior to experience; and they would have to be synthetic, rather than be mere empty tautologies, in order to possess a real content for knowledge. The substance of Kant's answer to this question—and thereby his answer to Hume's skepticism—is that the mind is an active and synthesizing organ, and that there are necessary patterns or forms in which it must organize its experience if it is to produce knowledge. Since they belong to the mind itself, these forms can be known a priori; and since they are the ways in which we *must* organize our experience, they can produce knowledge that is necessary rather than merely probable. The mind, in short, imposes its own patterns upon phenomena, which must conform to these patterns if they are to be admitted to consciousness at all. Things-in-themselves, outside the mind, might be altogether different from anything that we can imagine; but that would not prevent us from laying down certain laws as to what future experiences would be like, since those future experiences would have to have certain characteristics in order to enter the mind at all.

(Whether Kant has successfully answered the skepticism of Hume is not a question that concerns Heidegger. Nor is it a question that concerns us here. Indeed, Heidegger does not discuss the Kantian *Critique* at all as an attempt to secure the certainty of human knowledge. The question for him is what presuppositions about the nature of human existence Kant makes when he attempts to solve the knotty problems of human knowledge. These presuppositions sketch the foundations of an ontology of human existence, which it has been Heidegger's role to develop. To put it in another way: the question is what understanding of Being circulates between the lines and behind the scenes of the Kantian *Critique*.)

Kant's solution to Hume's difficulties might be quite satisfactory, if we could be sure that the forms of the mind would remain eternal and fixed. But this is just the point that the skeptic chooses to doubt, and the invariable question he raises against Kant is: Might not the mind change tomorrow so that I will apprehend things under altogether different and now unpredictable patterns? Bertrand Russell, with his usual nonchalance about historical accuracy, remarks that this difficulty is one of which Kant never seemed to be aware. On the contrary, Kant is very well aware of this difficulty, and he attempts to meet it in one of the most central, and also most difficult, sections of the *Critique of Pure Reason*, with the rather formidable title of "The Transcendental Deduction of the Categories." This section is also central to the Heideggerian interpretation of Kant.

The basis of this Kantian Deduction is the essential temporality of human consciousness. Suppose, Kant says in effect, the world or the mind should change so drastically that tomorrow experience comes at us higgledy-piggledy and at sixes and sevens. The disorder might be real disorder; still, our way of tracing some kind of order for ourselves amid the chaos would be temporal: we would try to note that regularly, or usually, after one experience, A, comes another, B. (We would have, in short, to use the category of causality.) Similarly: if this new kind of experience came to us in welters of qualities without any discernible things, or substances, we should still have to organize these qualities into some clusters that *persisted* as stable—that is, *endured relatively through time*—in relation to others that came and went. In short, we should be employing the category of substance and accident. We limit ourselves here to the two categories, causality and substance, which Hume's skepticism had most called in doubt. In both cases these categories, or strict analogues to them, must be employed by the mind insofar as the mind, essentially temporal, must project some temporal pattern upon phenomena.

The attempt might altogether fail in this curious kind of world we are imagining. The chaos might be real, and all attempts to find any kind of order might fail. But in that case consciousness itself, as a consecutive and meaningful process—that is, as something that is continuous in time—would also perish. Momentary blobs of consciousness, without a significant before and after, would not be a meaningful consciousness at all. Kant's deduction, then, is hypothetical to this extent: *if*, he argues, there is to be any order in experience, this order must involve at least some meaningful continuity of consciousness itself; and this last is possible only through the essential temporality of consciousness.

But this temporality of consciousness, for Kant, derives from something more fundamental than the specific nature of certain categories like substance and causality. It derives from the general nature of any human concept. A concept,

according to Kant, is essentially a synthesis of sense-perceptions. I look out of the window and see a tree; my concept "tree" implies that if I walk outside and touch the
trunk, I shall feel the solid bark; that if I walk to the other
side, I shall see leaves and trunk in a similar, though slightly
different, three-dimensional pattern; that if I wait several
months, I shall see the leaves turn yellow and drop one by
one in the fall; and so on and so on, for all the possible experiences that the tree may afford. My concept, tree, is what
binds together all these possible experiences in time. It is not
a concept of some essence over and beyond all these appearances but just the unifying synthesis, or structure, of all
these appearances. The concept, in short, is a temporal structure of experience.

By this radical interpretation of the nature of a human
concept,* Kant fathered three major movements within
modern philosophy: pragmatism, positivism, and the existentialism of Heidegger.

Charles Peirce, the American pragmatist, transformed
Kant's point into the view that the concept, as a synthesis, is
essentially a design, or plan, of action. What I mean when I
say, "there is a tree," is that I will act, or avoid acting, in a
certain way in relation to that particular object. Meanings
mean, as it were, a certain kind or pattern of behavior.
From this follow pragmatism and behaviorism.

The positivists seized upon the principle of verification

---

* Kant, of course, did not originate the idea. It came from British
empiricism, most notably from Berkeley's famous attack upon "abstract ideas"—viz., ideas which were empty because they had no correlated sense-perceptions. But Kant employed this principle more
systematically, and therefore more radically, than his British antici-
pators.

inherent in the Kantian view. A concept is meaningful if and only if there are possible sense-perceptions that will verify the presence or absence of the thing designated by that concept. In positivistic hands this becomes a weapon for cutting away the "meaningless" concepts of theology and metaphysics. Thus "the Absolute," "God," and a good many other traditional concepts are judged meaningless because there are no possible sense-perceptions that would verify the existence of these entities.

In contrast with these other scions of Kant, what Heidegger squeezes out of the Kantian view is the fact of *temporality* as providing the very possibility that there can be concepts, or meanings, at all. If I look out the window and say, "there is a tree," the word "tree" has meaning to me now only because my own being is spread out temporally in such a way as to encompass the possibility of all those particular future experiences in relation to the tree. Only a being whose being is essentially temporal can have concepts or meanings. Only because, at this very moment wherein I look out the window, my existence is beyond itself and so able to project a whole temporal horizon within which particular actions and verifications can be performed, can I think: tree. Heidegger here remains closer to Kant than do the other Kantian children, pragmatists and positivists: for he is dealing with temporality as the possibility presupposed by all particular (ontic) acts or verifications.

There can be no meaning without time—that is the momentous conclusion that Heidegger extracts from Kant. Extracts, not forces upon Kant; for the amazing thing is that Kant himself, not out of any existential pathos, but through an analysis of the human mind simply as an instrument of science, is led to place fundamental emphasis upon the temporality of consciousness. This means that man himself must be understood as an essentially temporal being. Kant thereby paves the way for an ontological analysis of human existence as essentially temporal and finite.

It would be a mistake to think that Heidegger has forced the conclusions of his own *Being and Time* upon Kant's *Critique*. Though the book on Kant did appear two years after *Being and Time*, its substance was already worked out in lectures that Heidegger had given at Marburg University some years before 1927. Indeed we have to think of the genesis of Heidegger's thought the other way about: it is the meditation upon Kant that leads him to the conclusions expressed in *Being and Time*. Heidegger's method is thoroughly historical and starts from the understanding of a text from the past. In this respect he is far closer to a philosopher like Hegel than to Husserl, and this kinship with Hegel becomes more marked in the later Heidegger. Husserl had attempted to found phenomenology as a discipline "without presuppositions," which would, in short, derive simply from the pure data of consciousness without anchoring itself upon the extraneous material of past philosophies. In actual practice this effort is illusory, for the philosopher, no matter how pure his thought, is always operating in some historical context, as Husserl himself in the contexts of Descartes and Kant. Man, as a radically temporal being, is also historical through and through, and his philosophizing is always caught in the toils of history. Philosophy itself therefore, as Hegel put it, is the history of philosophy. The genuine philosopher takes over the problems and contributions of the past and advances them a little further along the road that thought must travel. The fact that Heidegger is so deeply preoccupied with matters of textual interpretation is no denigration of him as an authentic philosopher, but, quite the contrary, a sign of his involvement with the essential historical fate of philosophy.

Heidegger's conclusions from Kant leave us with one final question for this section. If there can be meanings only because man is temporal, what then about a timeless or eternal being, such as God was traditionally supposed to be? This was the kind of question before which Kant confessed that his own mind grew dizzy. Heidegger chooses to remain scrupulously silent. He is satisfied to point out that the very conception of the eternal—as, for example, the "nunc stans," the ever-abiding now or present, in which medieval thought spoke of eternity—is projected, like all human meanings, from within the horizon of the temporal, and it has to employ the temporal "now" to express the state of being beyond all time.

No doubt, this view of temporality as the basic condition for all meaning will seem dismal to many minds because it seals man off from the eternal. In the ordinary experience of mankind time seems always to have figured as the destroyer: the devourer of youth and beauty, and the passage into old age, feebleness, and death. It is out of very understandable human motives that most philosophers from Plato onwards have sought an intellectual escape from the ravages of time into the changeless security of the eternal. But time is not merely the destroyer, it is also the producer of new and inexhaustible life. And temporality as the horizon of possibilities, more basic than time considered as mere succession, is a positive dimension of human existence: for it is that horizon in which man has to construct meanings and give his own individual existence meaning.

If, then, temporality is the condition for the possibility of any meanings whatsoever, it obviously provides the possibility of truth itself. Temporality is thus revealed as inextricably implicated with truth. We come back thus to the two basic meanings of "present" discussed earlier:

1) present as temporal, the present tense;
2) present as that which presents itself (truth).

The long analysis of Kant has thus brought us back to the simple, but so easily passed over, senses of the most ordinary word "is." The Kantian *Critique*, however much it would seem to have insulated itself in the purely epistemological analysis of concepts, turns out thus to be involved with the problem of problems: the meaning of Being.

# VI

## The Turning Point

THERE IS A RISK for the critic to speak of a turning point in Heidegger's thought. For nearly every position taken by the later Heidegger one can find a passage in the earlier work that prepares the way. Thus one could speak just as well of the remarkable continuity of this thought rather than of any abrupt turning point or points that it takes. Continuity and discontinuity in the case of any organic development go together and are complementary: from acorn to oak is one continuous process, yet what emerges at different stages of growth will be remarkably unlike what went before. The change in Heidegger is not at all a repudiation of earlier positions but an enlargement upon them. It is primarily a change in emphasis, in temper and tone. The later Heidegger is far more the historical prophet, his tone is more sweeping and apocalyptic, and the themes of his thought are the total historical perspectives of Western civilization.

Here are the central points in this change:

1) Metaphysics, and indeed philosophy itself, is finished. The earlier Heidegger had spoken of his efforts as a destruction of traditional ontology. But this destruction would itself be a form of ontology, which Heidegger called "fundamental ontology." Moreover, in the essay *What is Metaphysics?*, Heidegger thought of himself as still doing metaphysics, as the title itself of the essay shows. Twenty years later, in a foreword to this essay, he corrects this idea: his thought has gone beyond metaphysics altogether.

It should be remarked here, by the way, that when he speaks of metaphysics, and indeed of philosophy itself, as finished, he does not mean that thinking is finished; on the contrary, thought is merely in transition to a new historical epoch.

2) In *Being and Time* there had been two propositions that sounded paradoxical enough to provoke puzzlement and misunderstanding among many readers:

a) There is no Being (*Sein*) without man (*Dasein*); and
b) There is no "World" without man (*Dasein*).

At first glance these statements sound like the most extreme subjectivism, even solipsism. But of course Heidegger did not mean to assert that there would be no beings—no stars, planets, rocks, and trees—without man. Such a position would be a piece of colossal and arrogant philosophical egotism. Nor did he intend that the world, in the sense of physical universe, was the creation of man. His meaning, rather, was that Being as sheer presence—the Is of what-is —in its full temporal and historical concreteness is present only with man, or any other creature in the universe, if there be such, who is constituted by the possibilities of

*Dasein.* Similarly, there can be no world, in Heidegger's sense of world—namely as the total field of possibilities that man inhabits—without man, or some creature like him. In short, Being and World reveal themselves phenomenologically as structural components of the human Dasein.

But with all subjectivistic misinterpretations aside, these two propositions still carry a very marked emphasis upon man as the center of the whole field of Being. He is the creator and destroyer of worlds, as has been repeatedly shown in history through the emergence and destruction of very different world-perspectives at different epochs. The picture of man, or one part of the picture, that emerges from *Being and Time* is that of a creature who actively creates himself through his own projects: man is a self-projecting project. This is the aspect of his thought which Sartre fastens on almost exclusively and develops to the point where the human project seems to detach itself altogether from the background of Being. Given some (though not all) the emphases in his earlier work, Heidegger himself might have trod this path. It is most significant that he did not, and that the later Heidegger diverges even more sharply from the Sartrian brand of existentialism.

The emphasis of the later Heidegger is not upon man as the active center of Being, but upon Being itself as that which perpetually claims man. Man is not only *ek-sistenz*—the creature who actively transcends himself—but also an *in-sistenz*—a being who, however he may stand beyond himself, must always stand within Being itself. Man is not the Lord of Being, a creature who transforms and bulldozes the world of nature; rather, he is the shepherd of Being: the creature who carefully tends and guards Being in all its revelations. The first is the technician, the second the poet.

3) Consequent upon this last change there is a de-emphasis upon all assertions of will. Activity and human self-assertion have been the distinguishing features of Western civilization since the time of the Renaissance. By contrast, the Oriental civilizations, and even the earlier civilizations in the West, have been characterized more by a passive acceptance rather than the active will to transform nature. This overwhelming emphasis upon activity has found expression in the various philosophies of the will that have emerged within the modern period and reached their culmination in Hegel and Nietzsche.

To all of this Heidegger is opposed. This opposition does not mean that he wishes flaccidity and torpor to replace the will to action. In any case, the wheels of a civilization cannot be turned back by simple fiat. Activity and the will to action have resulted in the colossal achievements of modern times that we could not easily dispense with even if we really wanted to. The point is that the tremendous fever of activity of modern man can cut him off from his roots and launch him into the void. Activity, activity at all costs— that almost becomes the watchword in some sectors of modern society. Heidegger refers to this tendency within modern thought as *"the will to will"*—implying by this phrase that it ceases to be a concern what end is willed so long as the will itself is operative. What the late Heidegger persistently opposes to this frenzied "will to will" is the notion of "letting-be": at some point in the midst of his feverish drive to action man must learn to let-be if he is not to twist truth into the total distortions of some ideological fanaticism. To let-be is to let oneself be claimed by Being in its sheer presence. This is why the voice of the poet is so necessary in this time of need, and also why, Heidegger says in echo of Hölderlin, the poet is deemed useless in a spiritually impoverished time. This emphasis of the late Heidegger is conveyed through the title of a little book published in 1959: *Gelassenheit*—surrender or abandonment. That is to say, Being discloses itself to man only when, having given up the fearful claims of the will to action, he surrenders himself to the presence and the mystery of things.

These changes in Heidegger's views developed over a rather considerable period—from the late nineteen-twenties through the forties. In a sense, then, there is no dramatic turning point; if we have applied such a label in connection with the two essays—*What is Metaphysics?* and *On the Nature of Cause*—our point is that in these two works he had pushed certain views too far to continue to maintain them within the philosophical framework that he had already built up, so that in time he had to change the framework.

For example, in *What is Metaphysics?* he ends by describing metaphysics as "the fundamental happening within human existence." This, of course, is not at all the traditional sense of metaphysics as a discipline that aims to study being as being, what-is just insofar as it is. Heidegger was led into this characterization of metaphysics because he set out to describe man's encounter with Being as a living and dramatic event in human existence rather than a mere conceptual cerebration about the most general and empty of concepts. But once he had gone so far as to depict metaphysics in this way, he was bound to recognize that his thinking was not metaphysical at all and had in fact gone beyond metaphysics.

It is a rather ironical little coincidence that the positivist Rudolf Carnap published a severe criticism of Heidegger's essay, demolishing it for errors in logic and grammar, under the title: "The Surpassing of Metaphysics" (*Die Über-windung der Metaphysik*). Much later Heidegger himself was to publish an essay with the same title. Needless to say, the two destructions of metaphysics—the positivistic and the Heideggerian—have very little in common beyond their title. For Heidegger, positivism is still all too meta-physical—and without knowing it.

*What is Metaphysics?*, delivered as his public inaugural lecture at Freiburg, is concerned mainly with discussing the nature of the Nothing (*das Nichts*). On the face of it this must strike common sense as a perfectly absurd thing for a savant to be discussing publicly before a company of sa-vants. It must have been a strange and rather uncanny ex-perience at that time for Heidegger's hearers, the faculty and scholars of Freiburg University, to hear a discourse on this unlikely subject—a discourse, moreover, into which the lecturer flung himself with such passion and abandon-ment. But philosophers and "common sense," despite the present insistence of British philosophers, are not at all points essential bedmates, or the "common sense" of the ancient Athenians would not have judged Socrates to be such a monster and condemned him to drink the hemlock just for being odd and different. Philosophers are a queer breed, in the eyes of common sense, and they must be al-lowed to treat whatever strange subjects their roving and restless spirit leads them to. The question of Non-Being, moreover, has had an ancient, if somewhat hidden, place in the tradition of philosophy, beginning with Plato's elaborate discussion in his dialogue "The Sophist." Plato is led into that discussion not out of some antic spirit of novelty or oddity, but because the themes of his thought essentially lead him there: it is necessary to understand Non-Being if one is to understand the finitude of the particular beings within the sensible world.

Heidegger's discussion of the Nothing follows just as essentially from the themes of his own thought. His examination of Nothingness is not a frivolous play on words, but a serious attempt to confront directly certain modes of experience that are inescapable in human life: the negative is always present in the positive, and indeed, to put it somewhat paradoxically, the positive posits the negative as its very ground. Moreover, in the way it differs from the traditional account of Non-Being, Heidegger's derives from his own radically different understanding of Being, and helps us to understand this latter.

The traditional position, founded by Aristotle and solidified through centuries of Scholasticism, had regarded all negative being as purely mental or conceptual. According to this tradition, being (ens, that-which-is) is divided into two kinds:

1) *Ens reale*, a real entity, which has positive existence within the world of things (*in rerum natura*), like this table on which I am writing, or the tree there outside the window; and

2) *Ens rationis*, an entity of reason, a merely conceptual entity, like a centaur or a round square.

Thus all real existence is positive existence; the negative

has its place only in the human mind which can conceive and speak of things other than they actually are. The color non-green, for example, is not a real entity but a concept for all the colors that exist positively as yellow, blue, red, etc.—all colors other than green. And this holds true for all negative or privative modes of being: blindness, for example, as the absence of vision, is not itself a solid object in the world of things, and therefore is an *ens rationis*. It is, of course, a fact that a given individual may be blind, but the positive reality is a material growth over the eyes, a lesion in the optic nerve, or whatever other real entity, existing positively *in rerum natura*, makes impossible that form of *consciousness* that we call vision. There would not be such a thing as blindness if there were not consciousness; and this is the sense in which it would be listed as an *ens rationis*, an entity of reason.

So too, for example, with the *absence* of a dead person from a house where she has always lived with her family. That absence is not a real entity, like a physical body really present now within the house, however much that absence may haunt the survivors of the deceased. This absence is real only insofar as there are human minds that feel it. Hence it has reality only within consciousness; it is an *ens rationis*.

This distinction between the two modes of being is quite unexceptionable within the terms of its own analysis. For certain purposes of logical discourse it secures clarity and order; and it does get rid of certain intangible and somewhat ghostly entities that do not belong in the solid world of reality. It is, moreover, an analysis that is perfectly in line with one form of common sense.

Yet this disjunction between real and conceptual being harbors within itself the seed that blossoms as the dichotomy between object (*ens reale*) and subject (*ens cogitans*). Those who would make Descartes the villain for creating the Western dualism between subject and object ought to reconsider this judgment in the light of the traditional distinction between the two modes of being: the Cartesian dualism was already implicit within the traditional way in which Western philosophy conceived of Being. Real Being is what actually and positively exists, ultimately substances and their attributes; everything negative in experience—the so-called "negative facts" about whose status philosophers have so much debated—derives from human consciousness. But how then can the mind bring into reality something that is not found there without it? The mind becomes something intrinsically different and therefore alien from the substantial and positive things that exist outside it *in rerum natura*.

To understand the negative in experience we have then to go over to a radically different concept of Being. If we do not locate Being primarily in physical substances outside the mind, nor in the mind that apprehends data of which these physical objects may be the cause, but rather in the enveloping presence—the Is of what-is—that encompasses both thing and mind, then the disjunction between positive and negative being turns out to be provisional and useful but not absolute. This present situation in which I find myself surrounded by things is always penetrated through and through by the negative. This is particularly evident if we do not forget the temporal sense of the Is. This present moment, in which a world containing things and other people surrounds and grips me, is penetrated by the future, which is *not* yet, and torn from the past, which is *no* more. Thus the present, which traditionally has been taken as the real and actual point of time, is essentially constituted by two negatives. Therefore, the positive reality of the present is what it is through the negative of future and past that penetrate it. Moreover, the world as it presents itself is always indefinite and finite; and however far we may extend our horizon, beyond it there is always—Nothing. Readers of James Joyce's *Portrait of the Artist as a Young Man* may remember the passage where Stephen Dedalus as a young boy encounters Nothingness in trying to locate his own individual presence in the world:

He turned to the flyleaf of the geography and read what he had written there: himself, his name and where he was.

> *Stephen Dedalus*
> *Class of Elements*
> *Clongowes Wood College*
> *Sallins*
> *County Kildare*
> *Ireland*
> *Europe*
> *The World*
> *The Universe*

. . . Then he read the flyleaf from the bottom to the top till he came to his own name. That was he: and he read down the page again. What was after the universe? Nothing.

If this be deprecated as the mere naiveté of the child trying to draw imaginary boundaries to the world, it is on the other hand a naiveté that does not disfigure experience as it is given to us: no matter how we try to locate ourselves within the world, we do not escape the Nothing. We must always project the world against the background of Nothingness, and we ourselves are a human project within Nothingness. Heidegger, however, does not follow the path of Joyce's young hero in trying to locate Nothing as something that lies beyond the barriers of the world. On the contrary, since however far we go in trying to fix our place within the world the Nothing must be invoked, or if not invoked then left unspoken at the end of our address, this Nothing is therefore essentially involved with and internal to our human project of defining our world. The Nothing is not empty space outside the universe, but a possibility within human existence itself, insofar as this existence always projects its world.

This essential link between Nothing and World is also the link between the two essays, *What is Metaphysics?* and *On the Nature of Cause.* As the first is concerned with the Nothing, the latter deals with man insofar as he seeks a support or ground for his world. We have spoken of both essays as marking a turning point in Heidegger's thought, but it is the second that more clearly goes to an extreme toward which the early thought of Heidegger had been leading. For what he does in the essay, *On the Nature of Cause,* is to transform the traditional search by philosophers for a First Cause or Ultimate Ground of the universe into a search by man for some ultimate support to his own existence. Man is placed here more sharply and extremely at the center of the world than in any other of Heidegger's writings. For a thinker who has proclaimed that his thought eschews every form of subjectivism, Heidegger's point of view here seems strangely anthropocentric. It is, in fact, a form of Nietzschean humanism: Man, freed from the search for God, appears as the creator and destroyer of worlds. Man has taken the place of God. The later Heidegger was to go on and repudiate every form of humanism as incomplete and rootless, since it leaves unasked and unanswered the question in what man's humanity is to be rooted. For the later Heidegger, the figure of Nietzsche marks the end of Western philosophy, beyond which thought must slowly and patiently seek for new beginnings, because Nietzsche has gone to the very end and posed the question of humanism in its extreme and decisive form. But in this earlier essay, though the name of Nietzsche is not invoked, the perspective seems thoroughly Nietzschean throughout.

To be sure, a good deal of this is *sotto voce*. The quiet and academic tone of the essay masks the audacity of Heidegger's proposals. He begins, as if he were only another plodding professor, by citing passages from Aristotle, Leibnitz, and other philosophers that have to do with the notion of principle, cause, or ground. Then, without the fanfare of any announcement, he has transformed the whole theme into his own key. The metaphysical quest for a First Cause of the cosmos is transformed into a question of the "fundamental ontology" of human existence: of the *Dasein* that has within itself the possibility of grounding its own existence—though it must always be a ground that is incomplete and therefore involves the negative. (It is from this essay that Sartre derives his own dictum that man seeks to be God—i.e., seeks to establish an absolute ground for his own existence, but must perpetually fail.) Man takes the place of God, as he must in every form of humanism when pushed to its limit. But man, as this Nietzschean creator of his world, must always move within the Void. This is something that Heidegger, however much he may have moved toward Nietzsche in the year 1929, did not forget. The figure of Hölderlin, his complementary guardian angel, was to remind him that this Void, before which Nietzsche attempts such exuberance and bravado, is also the dark night of the world from which the gods have fled.

At any rate, after this essay Heidegger's thought ceases to have any kinship with anything we might call humanism, whether this humanism call itself "existentialist" (Sartre) or not.

# VII
## Truth, Freedom, Letting-Be

To REJECT HUMANISM in any form may strike the reader as a very inhumane thing to do. If somebody is not for humanism, then he must be against man. Such is the confusion created by propagandists who would make eternal a certain ideal that is in fact historically dated. The fact is that Western humanism is not the only interpretation of man that has been offered in the course of the historical civilizations. In relation to all the civilizations of the globe, this version of man happens to be a peculiarly local and even parochial one. Moreover, there are plentiful enough signs that it has lost its grip upon the imagination and enthusiasm of many people in our period—particularly the artists. Modern sculpture and painting either dispense with the human image, or else relate it, in some distorted or abstracted shape, to the non-human: to primitive sources of energy, to the world of rocks and trees and stones. Modern music offers almost as clear-cut an example of the same "de-humanization," for the music that is commonly called "atonal" takes us outside the comfortable and thoroughly humanized world of the great tonal music of the past. Even literature, which, enmeshed as it is in the requirements of character and plot, would seem to be tied irrevocably to the human image, has tended to multiply, disperse, and lose this image. For many people, of course, this loss of the human image is taken as a sign of enfeeblement of talent or confusion of purpose. But this is the judgment of people clinging to archaic modes; and it loses all cogency before the powerful and convincing quality of the works of art that it would condemn. The abandonment of a certain traditional "humanism" therefore does not mean a denigration of man but an extension of his being, and specifically an attempt to re-affirm his tie with the non-human in nature.

But ironically enough, while this movement beyond the "human" has been going on in art, the world of man has been spreading all over this planet and eradicating all other forms of life. Modern technology and modern medicine, with their accompanying population explosion, are now the dominating facts in the external social life of our time; and as such they have had a long historical preparation. Baudelaire spoke of "the tyranny of the human face" as a characteristic of the swarming city of the nineteenth century; modern technology is in the process of extending that tyranny all over the globe until the Sahara itself will some day be blanketed by levittowns and housing developments. Against this tide, certain works of modern art look like a desperate struggle for psychological compensation.

One must take into account both these opposed, and yet related, historical movements in order to grasp the full sense of Heidegger's repudiation of "humanism."

Since we have indicated the main emphases of the late Heidegger, we need not pursue a sequential examination of particular works. We shall, instead, discuss matters thematically, stepping where we need to from one work to another. In these late writings it becomes more difficult to isolate his themes separately and confine them singly to this or that individual work: as the thought becomes more unified and concentrated, all the Heideggerian themes tend to overlap in each work. However, the works that we shall draw on principally in this section are the three fairly brief essays—*On the Nature of Truth, Plato's Theory of Truth,* and *Letter on Humanism*—all products of the 1940's.

In dealing with the question of truth Heidegger begins, in his typical fashion, with the most banal and simple facts. If I make a true statement, its truth consists in a correspondence with fact. The statement "here is a table" is true because here, in fact, is a table. But how is it possible to compare a mental judgment with a physical fact, since these are two altogether dissimilar things? This question has plagued philosophers since the time of Descartes. Heidegger's way of cutting the Gordian knot is simplicity itself. If I take two coins, two half-dollars for example, and place one upon the other, they correspond, or match. This correspondence is possible because there is a field, or region, in which they meet and coincide: in this case, the simple space of ordinary experience. If, then, a mental judgment is to match a material fact, there must be a field or region in which the two can meet and coincide; and this field is Being itself, as encompassing presence, the region within which subject and object meet and which is in fact presupposed whenever we make this distinction. All philosophic attempts, no matter how intricate or ingenious, to explain how a mental state may know a physical fact, must presuppose this third presence, the open field in which the two have already met, and which itself is neither physical object nor mental concept. No philosopher beside Heidegger, however, has made this fact explicit.

Now, this openness of Being is precisely the primordial sense of truth as *a-letheia*, unhiddenness. Hence, propositional truth is possible only through the truth—i.e., unhiddenness—of Being.

But Heidegger, who had virtually pushed the analysis of truth this far in *Being and Time*, now brings something new into focus. To understand what truth is one must understand the possibility on which it is grounded. (Here again, as in Heidegger's earlier analysis, possibility is the basic fact for understanding.) Truth, he now tells us, is possible only through freedom—specifically, the *freedom to let-be*.

To base truth upon freedom looks at first glance either like a general truism (on the ontic level of fact) to the effect that researchers have to go their way unhampered by dictators, or else like a blatant paradox that would make truth dependent upon the human will. But neither of these interpretations expresses Heidegger's meaning. The freedom he is talking about is not the traditional freedom of the will, a characteristic of subjective volition. In the Heideggerian analysis everything subjective is grounded upon something trans-subjective—i.e., that goes beyond the dichotomy of subjective and objective. Thus the freedom he intends here is not a quality inhering in the individual subjective will but a possibility implicit within Being itself. The encompassing presence that surrounds me is already revealed to some extent; Being and truth are in this sense convertible, to use the traditional mode of speech though in an untraditional way; Being cannot be without revealing itself to some degree—that is, without letting itself be. Man, of course, can turn his back upon such revelation, can juggle and distort facts, twist and turn in the convolutions of his own rationalizations. But he may, on the other hand, surrender to the revelation that is there, and let-be. Thus this freedom comes, as it were, from a relaxation of the will rather than from its strenuous self-affirmation. In the traditional view, the freedom of the will, as an undetermined will, is something produced out of the will itself, somewhat like a man lifting himself by his own bootstraps; the freedom that Heidegger talks about is something that man *receives*, and that he can receive only by laying himself open to it. In a sense it is not *his* freedom at all: he has to be taken in its claim and gripped by it.

This view of truth rejects any notion that truth is fundamentally a human imposition upon the things that are. Truth may involve human judgments, systems, categories, schemata, etc.; but it resides in these only derivatively, not basically. However much all of this epistemological apparatus must be employed in gaining knowledge, the apparatus secures truth only if at some point man can let himself be in the presence of what is. The notion itself that truth resides primarily and basically in the human mind is for Heidegger a symptom of man's historical severance from Being. It is humanism expressing itself on the episte-

mological and metaphysical level. For what is humanism
but the effort to separate the human from the non-human
and accord a priority to everything that belongs to the
former?

This is the burden of one of Heidegger's most remarkable essays, *Plato's Theory of Truth*, and it is perfectly appropriate that he should have published this essay in the
same small volume with his explicit rejection of the humanism of Sartre, the *Letter on Humanism*. For the error of
Plato, according to Heidegger, lies in a humanism that accords to human values a pre-eminent reality over everything else that is. And for Heidegger, as for Whitehead, the
whole history of Western philosophy is Platonism in one
form or another, sometimes more and sometimes less disguised.

The nub of the matter lies in Plato's theory of Ideas. The
question what is the meaning of Being (i.e., what is the
meaning of Is) Plato has transformed into the question:
What are the things that are really real? His answer is that
these are the Ideas—the eternal essences that lie beyond time
and space and are grasped not by the senses but by the
intellect alone. But what is an Idea? Here Heidegger, in his
grubbing fashion, fastens on the etymology of the word:
ἰδέα in Greek is connected with the root verb for seeing, the
same root that appears in the Latin *video*, and in our English
*vision*. Thus an Idea, in its root sense, is an aspect or perspective. Every perspective, moreover, implies a human
point of view. Hence the "really real" things, the things to
which Plato accords a pre-eminent reality, are at bottom
human perspectives. Consequently, for Plato, truth ceases
to be the *a-letheia*, the unhiddenness of Being as it reveals

itself, which was the meaning of truth for the earlier
Greeks, and becomes instead the correctness (ὀρθότης) with
which the intellect grasps and manipulates its own perspectives.

Such a shift in the meaning of truth initiates the distinctly
humanist attitude of Western philosophy. Neither Chinese
nor Indian thought took this step of declaring truth to reside in the human intellect. Their emphasis is quite the
contrary, and they leave man thoroughly immersed in
Being. For this reason, perhaps, they were not able, like the
Greeks, to create science. The separation of man from nature was thus a great and necessary step forward in history,
but Plato takes this step by the audacious and dangerous
means of according to human perspectives a pre-eminent
reality over everything that is.

The orthodox Platonist may bridle at this interpretation.
He will point out that the Platonic Ideas are not mere concepts that exist only in the human mind but objective entities that *subsist* as real independently of human minds. To
be sure. But Heidegger, we may assume, is well aware of
this elementary thesis of orthodox Platonism that we are
taught in our introductory courses in philosophy. Now, it is
not quite clear that Plato had settled with himself the question of the independent subsistence of the Ideas (see the
*Parmenides*), and the *definite* doctrine of subsisting Ideas
quite clearly belongs to Platonism after Plato. But if one
takes the Ideas as subsisting realities and not as human concepts, one may very well ask whether one is not thereby
compounding the humanist fallacy. For what this Platonism
does is to take the mental concept, reify it, and grant it a
supreme and timeless reality beyond all the passing things of

this world. Here surely, certain human perspectives—the concepts of the intellect—have been accorded a pre-eminent reality.

Platonism enshrines the philosopher's professional prejudice to take only the objects of intellect as fully real. Consequently, it establishes within man a cleft between his intellect and the rest of his being. This Platonic dualism between intellect and senses, and hence between soul and body, has been decried so often that it is now a commonplace. What is original and profound in Heidegger's view is that he makes this dualism the consequence of a prior dislocation that severs man from the truth of Being by locating truth entirely in the human intellect.

He ends his essay on truth by pinpointing the progress of Western philosophy as a whole in moving on from Plato to St. Thomas Aquinas to Descartes to Nietzsche, the last of whom closes out the whole cycle.

1) Plato begins the cycle by locating truth in the "correctness" of the intellect and its ideas, forgetting the primordial dimension of truth as the unhidden and self-revealing presence (Being) in which we live, move, and have our being.

2) In the thirteenth century—which brought the earlier Middle Ages to an end by establishing the autonomy of human reason within its own sphere and firmly demarcating the separate fields of philosophy and dogmatic theology—St. Thomas Aquinas, discussing the meaning of truth in his *Quaestiones Disputatae de Veritate*, begins by asking: Is truth to be found in Being or in the human intellect? And he answers: In the intellect when it puts together concepts into judgments that correspond with things. The earlier

Middle Ages, on the contrary, following St. Augustine had thought of Being and truth as identical in the sense that all things in a universe radiant with the presence of God were truly what they were to the degree that they participated in that presence. St. Thomas is a considerable step forward in the precision and differentiation of thought; but what is already lost is the sense of the engulfing presence of the divine.

3) Descartes, in his own way a rather faithful scholastic, repeats the formula of Aquinas without any change: Truth is found in the intellect as it makes propositions or judgments.

But in the background of this formula things have changed, and some peculiar shadows rise. The world of the Greeks and the Medievals had been a simpler world that seemed to present itself as it really was so that the mind could know directly that its judgments corresponded with things outside the mind. But this older and simpler world had faded by the seventeenth century; the real world of "the new science" is very different from all appearance: the world of mathematical physics does not resemble the world of ordinary experience. Since appearance and reality are so very different, the doubt begins to dawn that perhaps the mind does not know things as they really are behind the veil of appearance. Ironically enough, Descartes rescues himself from this doubt by invoking from his medieval past the hypothesis of a God, at once benevolent and omnipotent, who created our minds so that they would "correspond" with the world outside. God is the ultimate guarantee that we may touch upon real truth.

4) When God dies this ultimate guarantee of truth disappears. So with Nietzsche the cycle reaches its apex and its reversal. Truth, says Nietzsche, is that form of lie, or fiction, that works and therefore increases our power.

Between Descartes and Nietzsche there lies the formidable figure of Kant, who had attempted to show that we cannot know things-in-themselves but only phenomena, or appearances. Therefore, says Nietzsche, let us abolish the thing-in-itself, we have only the flux of appearance. Here he speaks as ruthless positivist and pragmatist. Man may construct theories and explanations; we cannot know whether these correspond with things as they ultimately are; such theories and explanations serve only as tools that help us cope with the flux of becoming, and so because they foster the purposes of mankind, we call them true.

Here we move solely within the world of man, where the issue of power is dominant and the will to power defines the essence of man himself. This will to power expresses itself in the technological domination of the planet. Man no longer lives in harmony with nature, he transforms and conquers it, and ends by creating a thoroughly artificial and human environment for himself. This is unbridled and rampant humanism. But Nietzsche's greatness, unlike so many other "humanists," is that he does not play ducks and drakes with the ultimate consequences of his position but wills to go straight down the line to the end.

And it is the end. For with Nietzsche Western thought has reached the limits in which its own humanistic decisions enclose it. We may not wish to accept Nietzsche's desperate and violent tone, but the modern world stands where he indicated. The world of the eternal and the super-sensible has simply vanished as an historical fact, and we stand naked and alone in the world of man.

And the way out? Western thought, especially in this epoch that is dominated by physical science and technology, is not likely to relapse back into an Absolute or God. If there is a way out, there must be some other direction. This is what Heidegger hopes for, and what his thinking seeks to prepare.

Such is the thumbnail sketch of what Heidegger takes as the development of Western philosophy. To many it will seem altogether too simple and over-simplified an outline. But the simplicity of any explanation is not an objection provided the explanation can weave together all salient facts into a coherent whole. The history of philosophy, for Heidegger, is not isolated from the rest of human history. On the contrary, it is human history brought to its fullest revelation, so that what happens in philosophy is prophetic of what is to happen later in the rest of man's social and political life. Heidegger's interpretation of the history of philosophy thus entails a very definite interpretation of the whole history of Western civilization; and to this latter subject we now turn.

# VIII

## Historical Prophecy: The
## First and the Last

In *Being and Time* man is characterized as an essentially temporal being. This essential temporality of his existence is not an abstract chronometric time, but concrete and individual time, time here and now—in short, real historical time. Thus man as essentially temporal is also an essentially historical being; and every human action or project of thought is but a fragmentary gesture within the finite and circumscribed horizon of his history. It was to be expected therefore that Heidegger's thought, as it developed, would pass into that great area of the philosophy of history, cultivated by Hegel, rather than stay confined within the narrower field of Husserl's phenomenology. And this of course it has done: the theme of history is central to the later Heidegger, and whatever he attempts to interpret—whether it be poetry, the meaning of technology, or a pre-Socratic philosopher—is understood within his own bold and simple scheme for Western history as a whole.

Perhaps the time has arrived when philosophers can no longer escape the obligation of historical understanding. Every philosopher who has something to say opens up a new vista upon the whole past of philosophy and, consequently, since philosophy is an integral part of human civilization, upon the whole life of mankind in the past. And more than this: the bolder and more drastic his thought, the more it opens up new perspectives for the future. Since the future is the primary tense for Heidegger, it is also to be expected that all his efforts at historical understanding will involve his assuming the mantle of the historical prophet. This does not derive from any oracular bent that may or may not belong to his own private personality; it is a simple consequence of the fact that the attempt to understand the past always involves some project toward the future. Only man who is projected in some definite way toward the future can focus the energies of his thought meaningfully upon the past.

The modern philosopher has to think historically because history itself is rather a recent historical happening. What has come academically to be called the philosophy of history is a new development within philosophy. Its first glimmerings begin among the thinkers of the Enlightenment in the eighteenth century; but it does not come into being in any full-fledged form until Hegel in the nineteenth century. The ancients thought of history as a matter of cycles, the future repeating the past. To be sure, changes would occur; empires would rise and fall, the Persians give way to the Greeks and the Greeks to the Romans; but all these were individual variations within the same fundamental pattern. The sense of history, as it engulfs us moderns, begins only where there is a sense that the future, far from resembling the past, may be altogether different from it: that history, in short, has a direction. The Judeo-Christian scheme introduces such a sense of direction into history. Time does not move in cycles, but points irreversibly forward like an arrow, from the creation of the world out of nothing toward the Last Judgment that will finally separate the sheep from the goats, the saved from the damned, after which history ceases. But though time here has a direction, and history does move toward some goal, the direction is not one within history itself but a supernatural pattern imposed on it from without. So far as the actual life of man is concerned—in its social, technical, and even intellectual aspects —things will go on more or less in the same old round, while man in his moral life may wander closer to or further from salvation. In the eighteenth century, however, the notion of progress enters, and the thinkers of the Enlightenment interpret the pattern of history as a movement from the darkness of superstition to the light of rational and critical understanding. Here indeed, in all aspects of his life, man will have a future that is radically different from his past. The modern consciousness of history thus begins not so much from a new understanding of the past as from a radically different expectation of the future.

But only begins—for there is lacking one other essential ingredient in our contemporary consciousness of history: a sense of real anxiety before history. The historical vision of the Enlightenment is an optimism intoxicated with the possibilities of reason operating in all areas of human life: history will henceforth move onward and upward, if not always in an unvarying straight line, at least more or less continuously and without any catastrophic breaks or drops in the curve. This is still the basic view of the great historical visions of Hegel and Marx in the next century. For Hegel history is the movement of Spirit toward the full integration and possession of itself in freedom; for Marx, the movement toward the victory of the proletariat and the consequent destruction of all social classes so that man develops in full freedom within the classless society. Neither thinker is haunted by the possibility of radical fall or decline; there may be minor breaks here and there at some points, but the scheme in its totality is inevitable and not endangered by any radical contingency.

Only with Kierkegaard and Nietzsche in the nineteenth century does there arise the sense of the possibility of a radical decline in mankind's future, and with this the sense of historical anxiety that has obsessed our own century. Both these thinkers introduce the prospect of real contingency into history. If the future can be radically different from the past, it can be radically worse just as well as better than the past. A possibility to be is also a possibility not to be; every real contingency, like an ax, cuts both ways. One cannot have the luxury of believing in wonderful possibilities for the future of mankind without paying the price of anxiety for what those possibilities may become if they are misused. In our time this sense of historical anxiety has become enormously heightened by the development of thermonuclear bombs. But even if the shadow of the bomb were not around the corner, we would feel this sense of historical anxiety in the dizzying rate of social change that engulfs the individual today. Since Kierkegaard and Nietzsche this rate of change has not only accelerated, the acceleration itself has accelerated, so that there are moments when even the most "progressive" of us wonder whether mankind in this frenzy of change will not be uprooted too violently from its past. Any interpretation of history offered nowadays, no matter how "optimistic" its eventual prognoses, if it has not experienced this sense of historical anxiety, would simply fail to be contemporary. Cheap optimists may bask in the prospect of tomorrow's plastics and wonder drugs; but only those who believe in the greatness of man will be willing to accord to him the dimensions of possible tragedy, seeing him as the protagonist who can pull his world down in destruction around his head.

The Heideggerian interpretation of history seeks to be neither optimistic nor pessimistic but only lucidly detached about the possibilities for man. Compared with either Hegel or Marx, it will no doubt seem strikingly "pessimistic," but in its pessimism it may be a pretty good symptom of how far the twentieth century has traveled beyond the nineteenth.

As usual, Heidegger begins from the most ordinary and commonplace of facts. This compelling grasp of the commonplace, we have indicated earlier, is his hallmark as a thinker. For some hostile critics, however, this hold on the obvious is a cause for suspicion since when you boil Heidegger down, they say, you get only some commonplace. But the task of a thinker who is to interpret our time is not to seize upon some odd peripheral facts or some special gimmick of insight, but to lay hold of what is central and obvious and there for all to see if they had but a steady enough vision to keep their eyes upon it. It is always what is directly before our eyes that is the hardest to see, and precisely the easiest to forget when we start cerebrating in search of novelty. The point is not how commonplace Heidegger's data are, but how well this commonplace material becomes integrated into some unified vision.*

The central and dominating fact of our time is technology. This domination of technology is not merely a fact within Western civilization, but now holds sway over the whole globe as all peoples struggle to acquire technical mastery over their environment. Because of technology we have arrived at the first truly global civilization in history. Thus all the talk of historians like Spengler or Toynbee about civilizations as local and organic structures that have their own law of development and death fades into the past. A global civilization, in which technology makes possible the human domination of this planet, marks the entry of man upon a new historical epoch beyond that long epoch that spanned all the "higher civilizations" of the past. Man

---

* The materials of this section are derived from most of Heidegger's latest works, but particularly from two books: *Holzwege* (Paths in the Forest, 1949) and *Collected Essays and Lectures* (1954).

The title of the first work is a rather eloquent version of Heidegger's own conception of his role as a thinker: he is a ranger blazing trails in a forest. The trails in a forest may often look the same, but they are not really so. All, however, are within the same wood. That is to say, all his questions move within the same ultimate circle of inquiry, the question of Being. But if Heidegger should seem here to be puffing himself up by speaking of himself as a trail blazer, we may call to mind his other caution: sometimes in the forest a trail may peter out into nothing; and a trail blazer never knows whether the trail he is on may not be one of these that come to nothing.

has acquired a *domination over things;* and this domination is the central fact of his present history.

This mastery of things allows man to live more and more in an artificial and thoroughly human environment. Hand in hand with this technological development there goes the population explosion. This population expansion began in the countries that first experienced the industrial revolution, but it has now become worldwide. Modern medicine, which itself represents a triumph of technique, makes sure that more children live and more elders survive, so that the numbers of people on the globe increase even beyond what Malthus would have dreamed. Some population experts have calculated that in a century and a half each human being will have a couple of square feet of space to himself. This would be living in a thoroughly human world with a vengeance!

All of this is commonly labeled "progress." What else indeed can the triumphs of modern technology and modern medicine be called? Mankind now has available possibilities for more material goods, more comfort, more material health, than the past could ever have dreamed. Through the speed of modern travel and the power of modern communications all distances shrink. The planet does become *one*—and small. Through these means of travel and communication there is available for man a greater number of "experiences" than the past could know. But with all of these possibilities of consumption available, it does not seem that mankind is any happier than it was. Indeed, our epoch has been marked by a great groundswell of discontent directed at just these things that are commonly celebrated as progress. There are complaints that the machine will assimilate man to itself, or that modern civilization as a whole will swallow up what had been the humanity of man. The automobile disfigures the landscape. The number of automobiles makes traffic a snarling jungle within our cities. The mass media, with their slick stereotypes, dull the potentialities for individual expression. The modern world, in short, is going the way of Aldous Huxley's Brave New World or of George Orwell's 1984.

Heidegger does not find these complaints against modernity historically authentic. However moving they may be, or however accurate in their depiction of some of the more uncomfortable tendencies of modern society, they are complaints that do not alter anything. The writer who berates the machine will still find it necessary to take his Sunday spin in the automobile or hop from place to place in a plane. And certainly nobody would want to do away with modern medicine. Human history at this moment is in the grip of the drive for technique, and nothing can arrest it. Whatever our personal laments, we are all caught up in it.

And this will go on for a very long time, according to Heidegger. Such a long future perspective assumes, of course, that the bomb will not destroy our world. Though at the moment this is a very threatening possibility, there is a likelihood that as the bomb becomes easier and cheaper to make, and therefore available to more nations, the common danger will become more manifest and the weapon will not be used. In any case, the domination of technology within modern society has already begun to show the anachronisms of certain nineteenth-century ideologies. The antithesis of capitalism–communism, for example, cannot be taken as final and absolute. As technological advance becomes more and more necessary for national power, the U.S. government itself has had to finance such projects and so becomes an economic agent; and, on the other hand, if the Soviet Union is to grant its people's desire for more goods, it will have to adopt certain features of a consumer economy that are not fundamentally different from the capitalistic market. Needless to say, of course, word of this has not reached the political demagogues, who always thrive on the ideologies of a previous century.

All, or nearly all, the details in the foregoing picture are commonplace matters. It requires no great power of insight to see that technology alters the whole fabric of our life today. Heidegger's originality lies in the way he sees this fact as embedded within the whole history of Western philosophy. This historical vision is granted him because he takes philosophy itself as a central and decisive fact within Western history. The great philosophers are not merely idle speculators whose ideas may happen, in some passive way or other, to reflect the changes that are going on in the substratum of history; on the contrary, these philosophers project the future by laying down certain schemata of thought within the framework of which subsequent history plays out the details.

The present epoch of technology has had a very long philosophical preparation. Heidegger's whole philosophy of history is neither more nor less than an attempt to show what decisions within philosophy itself made possible the era of technology.

Technology is originally the product of Western civilization. It goes hand in hand with science, which is also a distinct product of the West. Neither religion nor art serves to distinguish East from West, since they are present in both cultures. Science has been developed only by the West. And this science begins with the Greeks. Why did the Greeks, and no other people, create science? The great and refined civilizations of China and India produced many extraordinary things, but they did not produce science. It cannot be argued that the Greeks happened merely to be more clever than these other peoples. Such a contention cannot hold water for a moment if we think of the extraordinary intelligence and practicality of classical Chinese civilization. No; the Greeks produced science because they were oriented toward it by their own philosophical conceptions, and the Chinese were oriented differently. Greek philosophy detached clear and distinct objects from the enveloping presence of Being, and made these into objects for rational research. Because the Greek philosophers began to grasp Being in a certain way, science became possible.

It is an historical truism, of course, that philosophy has been the mother of the sciences, and that disciplines like physics, chemistry, and biology were once parts of natural philosophy. In our own positivistic age, the children have grown so vast and arrogant that they threaten to oust the poor old mother altogether. But nobody seems to have squeezed the full juice from this historic commonplace as Heidegger has done. His point is that philosophy prepared the way by a certain conception of Being that made science possible. The Greeks initiated this objectification of Being: that is, the detachment of stable and recognizable objects from the encompassing presence that is Being itself. In the modern period, with the launching of mathematical physics, these objects are considered in their purely quantitative and measurable aspects. Descartes indeed proclaims that this aspect—extension—is the very essence of material objects. At the same time certain skeptical doubts arise as to whether the mind really corresponds with things as they are. So the mind itself, with its clear and distinct ideas, must become the locus of certainty. Ideas become more exact the more mathematically precise they are. Instruments of measurement become, as it were, extensions of the human senses: they certify a subjective idea as precise because it has been measured. Truth thus becomes something that cannot be understood apart from the humanly constructed instruments that make it possible. The extreme objectification of things leads to an opposite and equally extreme subjectivism. Physics becomes a science, as one physicist has put it, of pointer-readings: its truth is involved essentially with man-made and man-controlled instruments. And the need of such instruments comes out of the Cartesian doctrine of clear and distinct ideas, which in turn reaches back historically to the original Greek detachment of distinct objects within Being.

Thus there is nothing fantastic about Heidegger's speaking of a single epoch in the history of man extending from Anaximander, the earliest Greek philosopher of whom we have a fragment, to Nietzsche in the nineteenth century and our own contemporary technological situation in this century. After all, the seed always looks disproportionately tiny in comparison with the full-grown plant. The fact remains that if those early Greek thinkers had not taken the steps they did the West might have developed along the lines of China or India. One finds in Lao-tse or the Upanishads another kind of wisdom, which does not prepare the mind for science.

Heidegger speaks of this Western development as the history of Being. He must be taken literally here: it is Being itself that is undergoing, or projecting itself in, this history. One may make a first approximation to Heidegger's meaning here by considering that in every epoch there are underlying presuppositions as to what beings are real and what the fundamental characteristics of those beings are. Thus in every epoch there is at work, whether noticed or not and more often unnoticed than not, a fundamental conception of Being. This is true even for the most positivistic of positivists, however much they may dissimulate their metaphysical presuppositions. History, then, involves the successive epochal conceptions of Being, within the framework of which man works out the details of his life. But to stop at this point is to remain at a subjective level, and Heidegger seeks to transcend subjectivism in all its forms. The fact is that man's subjective conceptions of what beings are real is a consequence of how Being has revealed itself to him. His conceptions express those aspects of Being that have taken him in their grip, and to which, consequently, he accords paramount importance and reality. These aspects are what he takes as "really real," in Plato's phrase. The "really real" for the modern mind is the fact that is objective, measurable, quantitative. The first step in the long history that has brought us to this point was taken when this aspect of Being, or the possibilities of it, took the early

Greek thinkers in its grip, and other aspects were let recede and were forgotten.

If it has taken 2500 years to traverse the distance from the early Greek thinkers to our present era of the technological domination over things, then we must expect, Heidegger says, that this present era will last an equally long time. This present of ours, according to Heidegger, is the evening of the West—an evening that ushers in a long night before there will be another dawn. And this night will last very long.

To call it a night is not to deny it all the positive aspects that would enchant the most "progressive" of minds. Though philosophically the possibilities of this era are exhausted, and there will be no more sweeping or new speculative philosophies or theologies, the possibilities *in detail* of technology and science are limitless. Already our new gadgets and contrivances make the machines of the past look archaic, and this process of improvements upon details will continue. Medicine knows no fixed horizons. Heretofore man has transformed nature in the inorganic realm that lay outside him, but now medical technology prepares itself to enter upon a new stage: to tamper with and transform human biology itself. Everything else being equal, the level of human health in the future should make the past look sick. Man, emerging as the master of Being, may even develop the technique for directing his own biological evolution. Let us hope that he will choose wisely the way in which to direct it.

Naturally, amid this extraordinary triumph of technique there will be some dark spots for those who retain some attachments to the past. As objects become more purely objective, they cease to have human associations: the family car or TV set are replaced when consumed; they do not become family heirlooms; and this will be true of modern furniture, plastic dishes, and even houses themselves designed as "machines for living." Housing developments will provide more efficient living conditions for ever greater masses of people; but there will be a vast uniformity in the cities of tomorrow that will remove the individual charm or sense of the past in old houses. An old machine—if we think of a house as a machine for living—is something that does not function and has to be replaced. Already a city like New York has transformed itself into something that cannot preserve its past. It is an ironical paradox that the speed of change, which originally engendered the sense of history, may become so great and automatic that people may lose the historic sense altogether. They will live in the present of ceaseless technological change.

Naturally, nature too recedes before the human. Here and there small enclaves will be left by law in the form of parks or wild life preserves, but one can imagine the day when the population pressure will be such that there will be agitation for housing developments within Yellowstone Park. What will happen to the birds and the animals? Already the game in Africa is disappearing as the human animal begins at last to dominate that once intractably dark continent. With modern means of technology, and a determined will, all the backward regions of the earth could be industrialized within a decade.

What is lost, as nature disappears, is the sense of Being as presence, the realm inhabited by the poets. Awe, the sense of mystery, and the reverence for mystery, which some archaic minds still feel in the presence of nature, disappear in the modern world. With this disappearance the objectification of Being—this immense achievement of millenia—has reached its culmination. The object considered purely as object—the TV set in a room of modern machine-made furniture—is strictly functional, and it is not a *thing* invested with a presence that evokes the language of the poets.

So we come back to the point from which this essay started—Heidegger and the poets, secret kin in their uneasiness before the modern world. The historical perspective of the late Heidegger, though it traverses its own particular pathways of thought, moves within the same domain as the malaise of the modern poet.

Yet it would be a mistake to think that the Heideggerian malaise remains merely an attachment to an archaic mentality. Even here, where his perspective seems darkest, possibility remains the basic fact for human reality. The silent power of the possible is still at work in man. At the end of the long corridor of night some other possibilities may reveal themselves to man, and human civilization may take a new turn. These will not be possibilities in the sense of some new spectacular gadget or specialized scientific theory—which would be only details within the old framework. Nor will it be any new theory within philosophy, which is exhausted and can only manufacture new and more trivial items of debate within the old framework. These new possibilities will have to be changes in the total outlook of man. They will be products of a more fundamental kind of thinking than technical or metaphysical cerebration—a thinking that descends into the poverty of its own past in order to issue in a new future for mankind.

At the end of the long corridor of night a crack of light shows beneath the door.

# IX

## On the Way Toward Heidegger

WHAT IS ONE to think of this perspective? Certainly the central fact with which Heidegger is attempting to grapple should give every reflective person pause: that the present is a period of transition beyond the past as drastic as— perhaps even more drastic than—the passage of primitive man into the ancient higher civilizations. In the nineteenth century Nietzsche had already grasped this startling transformation of man—which is one reason among others that the thought of the late Heidegger revolves so much around the Nietzschean riddle. An historical change as broad as Heidegger's raises so many questions that we can hardly sum up the pros and cons in a neat package. We who are caught up in this change may never be able to make such a tidy assessment. In any case, the thought of Heidegger needs still to be assimilated and pondered, and our purpose here has been simply to advance this assimilation.

That is why we finish this exposition on the note, echo-

ing one of his own titles: "On the way toward Heidegger."
To produce a ready refutation, or indeed a ready approba-
tion, of a doctrine is easier than to dwell with a thinker and
let his thought take possession of one. The reader who compares the two parts of this book will observe that this writer
has become much more cautious and tentative in his criticisms of Heidegger. One learns in living with the thought
of a thinker that a good many of one's initial refutations,
however clever, are not really cogent. It is salutary to find
one's own way in thinking by following patiently the
thought of another man and letting it be. This is the way
of Heidegger himself in his own interpretations of other
philosophers. A philosophic doctrine is never repeated in
exposition; it is recreated. The present writer does not
know for sure where in this essay his own insight has transformed or developed Heidegger. What Heidegger suggests
in his interpretations of other philosophers is undoubtedly
right: namely, that we have really assimilated another philosopher's thought only when we have already thought beyond him. Such a claim by an interpreter of Heidegger
would be not only arrogant but absurd, since the thought
of this philosopher, in his eightieth year, is still on the way.
A 1600-page book on Nietzsche has just been published! So
we must content ourselves with the more modest claim that
we are only on the way toward Heidegger, and that the
foregoing notes may be of some use to help others along
the same path.